AS I LIKE IT

AS I LIKE IT

Karan Thapar

First published 2018

ISBN 978-81-8328-466-0

Published by
Wisdom Tree
4779/23, Ansari Road
Darya Ganj, New Delhi-110002
Ph.: 011-23247966/67/68
wisdomtreebooks@gmail.com

Printed in India

For my three sisters,
Premila, Shobha and Kiran, with love

Contents

Preface xi

Entertaining Encounters

1. How Prince William Hit Sachin for a Six and Joked about It 3
2. One Does Not Get to Know Hollande until One Meets Him 5
3. Kiss Me Kate 7
4. Remembering Ravi Shankar 9
5. Sachin is Special because He's a Good Man 11
6. A Rewarding Encounter 13
7. Leander Paes 17
8. Not Quite Cricket 19
9. Did You Know? 21
10. Katrina Kaif 24

'Delights' Of English Language

1. English Richness 29
2. Under a Spelling 31
3. Thank You, Miss Truss 33
4. The Joys of English! 36
5. Unbelievable Words 39

'Daylights' Of English Language

1. English, as She's Spoken and Written 45
2. The Fun of Being Wrong 48

3. The Words We Use 51
4. Use of English Language 54
5. What an Idea, Sirjee! 57

The 'Literary' Affairs

1. Eternal Vigilance is the Price We Pay for Our Liberties 61
2. An 'Accident' that Gave Him the Post, Not the Power 63
3. To Natwar with Love 65
4. Writing about Yourself 67
5. Jaswant and Jinnah 69
6. King Charles III 71
7. The Literary Indian 73
8. Why I Like Khushwant Singh 75

No Offence Please

1. Let's Face It: We, Indians, are a Highly Racist People 81
2. Disadvantage India 84
3. Oh, to be in England Cracking Jokes about the Queen! 87
4. Richard, Shilpa and Young Mr Gandhi 89
5. Shame on Us! 92
6. To Our Politicians—Please Stop! 94
7. Grace in Defeat, a Lesson from Britain for Indian Politicos 97
8. We Need Cricketers Like Sachin but Definitely Not MPs! 99
9. When It Comes to Our Chaps, the Joke's Never on Them 102

The 'General' Idea

1. A Question of Generals 107
2. Fluffy Pillows, Peanut Butter and General Pinochet 110
3. Jacob's Jewels 113
4. The Charm of the Generals 115
5. The Weekend of the Generals 119
6. The Major and the General 123

Strictly Politics

1. Why Modi of 2017 is Not Modi of 2014 129
2. Advantage Mrs Swaraj 131
3. The Importance of Being Shashi Tharoor even if Congress Disagrees 133
4. Modi's Right, Do Not Politicise Triple Talaq 135
5. Suspension of MPs: A Very Healthy Precedent Set 138
6. Cry My Beloved Country—or Not? 141
7. Trying All the Wrong Things before Doing the Right One 143
8. Modi and Dress Diplomacy 146
9. A Case of Two Donalds but One Quack! 148

Women In Power

1. The Iron Lady 153
2. Can Women Make their Own Luck? 155
3. Sheila Dikshit 158
4. Indira Gandhi 161
5. Understanding Mamata 163
6. The Lady's Fingers 165
7. The Price of Politics 168

Wit On The Rocks

1. A Bit of This and That 173
2. The Art of Being Witty 175
3. Wit and Whisky 178
4. Words, Words, Words 180
5. Welcome King Freddy 183
6. The Sting is in the Tail 185

Sartorial Issues And The Barber Philosophers

1. Mr Sinkins' Buttons 189
2. Oh, to be Bald! 192

3. Pritam, the Philosopher 195
4. What an *Aam Aadmi* Can Teach the Chief Minister if Mr Kejriwal is Willing to Learn? 198
5. When Your Problem Lies at the Bottom 200

Portrait Of A Mother
1. Indrajit Gupta and Mummy 207
2. The Army Way 210
3. Doctors with a Difference 213
4. When Jest is Best 216
5. Never Say Die 218
6. Mother Knows Best 220
7. Mummy @ 94! 222
8. Remembering Mummy 224

Appendix
Can You Trust a Newspaper? 229

Preface

In July 2017 *Sunday Sentiments* turned twenty years old. It can now claim to be an adult column! However, the elements of juvenility that you can frequently glimpse in this collection are, I believe, a true reflection of my personality. I'm a child at heart. For some, in fact, a spoilt brat. The moments of sententious pontification—and I have to admit there are a few—may come easily but they are not really me.

Sunday Sentiments began as a diary. The first, on 6 July 1997, boastfully recounted a dinner with then Prime Minister Inder Gujral. I couldn't hide the fact I was delighted to have been invited. Sadly, beyond that point and a few other details, I didn't have very much more to report. Showing-off was my intention and purpose!

Over the years *Sunday Sentiments* has developed in many directions. First, it's travelled right across the *Hindustan Times*. It began on the outer page of one of the weekend supplements. This was its home for almost a decade. At this stage, it was largely a diary but struggling to become a proper column. That is to say the number of items kept shrinking whilst the length of each was steadily growing.

Then, developing wandering feet, it entered *Brunch*. I'm not sure why but that was only a temporary halt. Perhaps feeling out of place, *Sunday Sentiments* fled the magazine for the op-ed pages of the main paper and there it has stayed ever since.

It was here that *Sunday Sentiments* developed the form it's had for the last decade. It became a single issue column although its length, under pressure of space, kept shrinking. But the column you're familiar with dates back to this period.

The second development which also happened on the op-ed pages is that *Sunday Sentiments* became an eccentric if not idiosyncratic column. It became the vehicle for both my serious reflections on major issues of the day but also an opportunity to ventilate quirky ideas and even, occasionally, jokes and frivolous thoughts.

Either way the aim was always to inform or entertain. Rarely was it to preach. Indeed, when expressing an opinion became inevitable—or irresistible—I tried to do so by raising questions that would prompt the reader to the conclusion I was pushing at rather than assert it upfront.

Did I succeed? I'd like to think so and often, when people asked about my political views, I felt I had because that suggested they were unable to glean them from what I had written. But my critics were always sure they knew and they weren't always wrong.

I'm proud I haven't missed a single one of the 1040 columns over the last two decades although, to be honest, one was submitted but never published. That particular piece criticised the *Hindustan Times Diary* (written, I believe, by the then editor Vir Sanghvi) for a rather vicious but wholly inaccurate attack on an interview I had done with Kapil Dev for the BBC. The editor refused to use it but agreed to accept an alternate column in its place. I refused to give him one and preferred to go unread that week. This was way back in May 2000. Nothing similar has ever happened again. That article has been included in this collection as the appendix.

The lighter columns introduced the readership to my friends, and often, to those who had impressed me. There was Pritam and, many years later, Rajesh, both barbers at the Taj Mahal Hotel. There was Pappu, the young marker at the Gymkhana Club. And then there was Pertie. He's featured in more columns than any other single person. I've used him as a foil or alter ego, as a spokesman and even, at times, as a way of accepting my own mistakes by giving him the power to admonish me.

For some reason that I've never fully fathomed, Pertie struck a chord with many of you. Several read themselves into the stories about him. Some even questioned whether he was my creation. On a few occasions, when readers of this column actually met Pertie, they were quite flabbergasted. The one that stands out was when I introduced him at a party and the response was 'Good heavens! I always thought you were fiction'.

However, the columns that attracted most attention or, at least, comment—and certainly got me the biggest response—were about Mummy. That was the name by which I wrote about her. I don't think I ever revealed her actual name although I've written about Mummy in many different circumstances and for a multiple variety of reasons. For instance, I wove her into stories about Atal Bihari Vajpayee, recounted her memories of her presentation at Court in the 1930s, and remembered her joie de vivre and her often rebellious spirit in the obituary I wrote when she died at 98 in 2015. Some of those columns are part of this collection. She is no longer with us but I hope they capture her spirit and her personality which deserves to endure.

This is the third collection of *Sunday Sentiments* columns to be published as a book. The first was simply called *Sunday Sentiments*. The second, with possible reference to my greying hair, was called *More Salt Than Pepper*. Mostly, this collection has been put together by the publishers of this book. I thought it would be best if they, rather than I, should exercise editorial judgement and decide what to include and what to keep out.

I hope you enjoy reading these columns as much as I have enjoyed writing them.

Entertaining Encounters

1

How Prince William Hit Sachin for a Six and Joked about It

It might sound odd but I feel like a line in a famous song from the 1920s: 'I've danced with a man, who's danced with a girl, who's danced with the Prince of Wales.' Herbert Farjeon wrote this in 1927 at the height of the popularity of Edward, Prince of Wales, who briefly ruled as Edward VIII.

It popped into my head as I stood with some thirty others in a circular line in the British high commissioner's drawing-room to be introduced to the Cambridges. Before Sir Dominic led them to the sweating masses in the garden, he put aside forty minutes for an eclectic selection of Indians.

Now in England they say punctuality is the politeness of royalty. The Queen, I am told, is always on the dot of time. I guess in deference to our Indian habits her grandchildren were half-an-hour late. But that hardly mattered. Expectation only made our hearts grow fonder.

The first thing you notice about the Cambridges is their height. He is well over six feet and she is only an inch or so shorter. The next striking feature is their smiles. Both were flashing radiant ones whilst her eyes seemed to twinkle as well. They are quite mesmerising.

Finally, no one missed how incredibly elegant and thin the Duchess is. The first was expected but the second was everyone's initial comment after she moved on.

Maneka Gandhi, who was standing beside me, whispered: 'I can't believe a mother of two, whose last child was born eleven months ago, can be so thin.' Jitendra Singh, the Minister in the PMO, nodded in agreement. That reminded me of something 'Mrs. Simpson' (later Duchess of Windsor and the woman for whom Edward VIII abdicated) is alleged to have said: 'You can't be too rich or too thin!'

Now small talk is never easy and it certainly doesn't come naturally. However, it literally trips-off the Cambridge tongue and I mean that as a true compliment. To chat with thirty strangers isn't easy. On top of that to look genuinely interested and appear to enjoy it is a truly royal talent. Plebs don't have it.

When it was my turn, Dominic introduced me as someone who wanted to interview Prince William and added: 'I didn't let him!' It provoked a guffaw. 'He's protecting me!' the Duke riposted.

We first chatted about the King and Queen of Bhutan, who he was due to meet a few days later. 'I tell you what,' Prince William said with a large smile and a wicked look in his eyes. 'll get you an interview with the King and the high commissioner can't stop that!'

Next, cricket and Sachin Tendulkar, subjects on which I am no expert. Nor, I suspect, is the Prince. 'I gather you hit Sachin for a six yesterday?' I said. 'I did indeed and, let me add, it was one of his faster balls.' Everyone started laughing.

The Duchess obviously heard her husband's joke. 'What he didn't add is he got out on the next ball!' Unfortunately, that's all I can remember of my two minutes. I know we chatted about other things but I was transfixed by her elegance and bewitching eyes. I guess I was star-struck!

So, now, you know why I began the way I did. The Herbert Farjeon song revels in the then Prince of Wales. Ninety years later I'm reveling in his great great niece and nephew. Let me, therefore, borrow from the song once again:

'My word I've had a party, my word I've had a spree, believe me or believe me not, it's all the same to me! I'm wild with exultation, I'm dizzy with success, for I've danced with a man, who, well, you'll never guess...'

2

One Does Not Get to Know Hollande until One Meets Him

You only get to know a man when you meet him. Although we're all aware of this truism it hasn't stopped many from forming unshakable opinions of people they don't know. And when it comes to politicians what we read in the papers or see on television is sufficient to usually conclude we don't like them.

On Republic Day 2016, I discovered how mistaken we can be. Till then I had judged Francois Hollande by his appearance and the *Financial Times* criticism of his economic policies. He's short and squat, has no neck, wears big glasses and seems a little awkward. To this unappealing description the *FT* added a stinging critique of his decision to increase tax to 75 per cent for the super-rich, driving the actor Gerard Depardieu out of the country and provoking French football clubs to go on strike.

I think it's fair to say Hollande isn't considered the politician people would most want to meet. Well, they're terribly wrong. Though the sad part is until they meet him they won't know it.

I recently had that good fortune. The French President was invited to a private lunch by my old school chum Analjit Singh and I was one of the thirty other lucky guests. All of us were excited. Who isn't when you're about to meet one of the most powerful men in the world?

However, what none of us knew was how big a surprise lay in store. Hollande is charming and chatty. His conversation is informal, informed and interesting. His presence is inviting and not the least bit intimidating. In short, he is an extremely nice and likeable man.

On his arrival the French Ambassador—another Francois but this time surnamed Richier—introduced the President to everyone. No doubt Hollande was brilliantly briefed but he used it to astonishing effect. He chatted effortlessly about subjects connected to each of us.

In my case he recalled an interview I requested which he had been unable to fit in. But he referred to it with a delightfully wicked touch of humour. 'I'm told saying no was the wise thing to do. I believe Mr Modi once walked out, but if I did that the French press would crucify me.' The smile that followed was bewitching.

Before lunch the President walked from group to group, often on his own, to talk to different sets of people. He listened avidly, smiled a lot, laughed often and made them laugh a lot more. He seemed to have all the time in the world.

At lunch Francois Richier asked me to sit at the President's table. There were just five of us. Hollande asked questions about politics, terror, books, the media, cricket and youth fashion. He seemed genuinely curious. But what fascinated us was his account of the terror attack at the Stade de France last November. He told it like a story, graphically and grippingly. Everyone stopped eating, listening intently to every word.

In between, there were MPs wanting selfies, authors bursting with pompous advice on tolerance and a few loud braggarts out to attract attention. In each case Hollande good-naturedly played along. He even seemed pleased by their outbursts or interruptions.

When it was time to leave—and he was already out of the dining room—he walked back to shake my hand. 'If you ask again I may not say no!' he smilingly added.

Monsieur Hollande can be certain I will.

3

Kiss Me Kate

I was twenty-one when I first met Dev Anand. I was an undergraduate at Cambridge. An acquaintance in London telephoned to ask if I would show the actor around and more out of curiosity than enthusiasm, I agreed. I knew who Dev was but I was untouched by his fame and unfamiliar with most of his films.

Dev arrived early the following Sunday. I was still in bed. But my unpreparedness got our relationship off to a rollicking start. I offered coffee and croissants whilst I hurriedly dressed.

'What time do you normally get up?' Dev innocently asked, as he saw me hunting for a clean shirt and digging my jeans out from under the bed.

'Midday,' I replied.

'Oh dear, I've cost you three hours of sleep!'

Dev had come to Cambridge with a specific purpose in mind. He was on a recce for *Des Pardes* and looking for an Indian boy and an English girl who he would film canoodling by the banks of the Cam as a sort of leitmotif for the film.

We spent the day together. Dev was fascinated by the university town. We lunched at the Copper Kettle on King's Parade, visited the Union, punted on the Cam—where he nearly fell into the river—and strolled along the Backs. Kat Allinson, a dear friend whose father happened to be deputy high commissioner in Delhi, kept him in splits with her insouciant humour.

'So, will you two do it for me?' that's how he popped the question just before boarding the taxi for the station. Chuffed at the prospect of becoming 'stars', we agreed.

A week later, Dev was back. Kat and I were made to sit by the river and asked to kiss. It wasn't the two of us that attracted the crowd. The crew did that.

At first being asked to do it again seemed like the perfect excuse for more. But when it became clear the cameraman disapproved of our lack of ardour and, very possibly our inexperience, it started to feel ludicrous. Worse, the undergraduates ogling us were shouting instructions on how to do it which Dev echoed with gleeful delight.

Alas, when the film appeared our clinch was reduced to a fleeting shot tucked under the titles. When I first saw *Des Pardes* I missed it. The next time, I needed a friend to point it out.

But Dev became a friend. On subsequent visits to England he'd invite me 'and all the friends you can find', to lunch at the Carlton Towers. I discovered he loved strawberries and cream, even in winter when they're fiendishly expensive! And nothing made him happier than watching hungry undergraduates eat.

Twenty-five years later, he was my guest on the BBC interview *Face to Face*. 'Tell me,' he asked, 'do you want the truth or do you want an act?' Not sure which would be better, I opted for both.

Dev delivered in spades, except you'd never have guessed where one ended and the other began. He spoke of his mother: 'I loved her more than anyone else'; Suraiya, his 'calf love' and how breaking up made a man of him; and Kalpana Kartik, who he married during a lunch break. He joked about the caps he adored, revealed details of the diary he kept since 1945 and described himself as an eternal optimist.

He ended promising to write his autobiography. 'It'll just take four weeks,' he said. But did he keep his word?

Remembering Ravi Shankar

Although he was unaware of it, my first moment of what I think of as fame—if you'll permit a little blowing of the old trumpet—was because of Pandit Ravi Shankar. It happened in January 1977. I was president of the Cambridge Union and determined to do something out of the ordinary to ensure I was remembered.

What I hit upon was a Ravi Shankar concert at King's College chapel to raise money for Oxfam. The Union had never seen anything like it before. Nor had Ravi Shankar.

It was fixed for 30 January which turned out to be the coldest day of the year. Although over a thousand crammed into the chapel, perfumed for the occasion with joss sticks, the venue was unheated. The stone floors and towering stained-glass windows only enhanced the chill.

'We're going to have to play furiously to warm this place up!' Panditji quipped, moving a collection of lit joss sticks a little closer in the hope they might offer some heat.

What followed was entrancing. Panditji was accompanied by Alla Rakha and Prodyot Sen. Encouraged by the unique setting and the enthusiastic response, they played past midnight. As the evening reached its climax, the heavens opened and it started to snow!

I'm not sure if, thirty-five years later, the Cambridge Union still remembers the occasion but, at the time, it was the talk of the town. Both the local *Cambridge Evening News* and the London-based *Guardian* carried pictures on their front pages showing Panditji playing in the chapel in the precise position where the altar should have been.

The next time I met the sitar maestro was in 1983 at a special television concert for *Eastern Eye*, a programme I helped produce. On this occasion, however, Panditji's music created a unique problem for the director, Mike Toppin. 'What do you mean the piece he's playing can change depending on his mood?' he asked, unfamiliar with the influence of improvisation on Indian music. 'How can I direct the cameras if I don't know what's happening?'

Try hard as I did to explain, Mike's dilemma only got worse. I could sense his mounting exasperation. Fortunately, Panditji stepped in the day before the concert.

'Sit with me Mike,' he said, gently patting the area on the floor beside him. Over the next half hour he explained how Indian music worked. In turn, Mike explained the grammar of television studio direction.

'I'll tell you what,' Panditji suddenly said, 'I'll play the raga I'm going to play tomorrow and you can record it on your little tape recorder. I promise you it won't be very different at the concert.'

Panditji and Mike worked out a secret arrangement to indicate to the uninitiated Englishman when the alaap would end. If I recall correctly, it was a nod to camera three. Till then the focus was firmly on him and the sitar. Thereafter, six other cameras came into play.

My third and final meeting was seventeen years later at an interview for the BBC. When I introduced myself, he interrupted with a big hearty laugh. 'How can I forget that night in Cambridge when you gave Alla Rakha sausages to eat claiming you didn't realise he was a Muslim!'

Then, when he saw my face fall, he added: 'This time you're going to come to my home and meet my family. I've told them all about you.'

I remember that dinner very well but sadly, we never met again.

5

Sachin is Special because He's a Good Man

I don't understand cricket and to be honest, I don't really like it either. Consequently, I don't know very much about Sachin Tendulkar.

However, I've always sensed there's something special about him. The problem is I wasn't sure what till my sister, Premila, put her finger on it. 'He's a good man,' she said. For many that would be putting it too simply. But it has the ring of truth.

When I call Sachin good, I'm not talking about his cricketing competence or any saintly streak in his character. I'm referring to certain niceness, a likeability that quickly communicates itself.

For instance, I don't think Sachin has ever bragged. At his press conference, the afternoon after his retirement, there was a candour and sincerity that was winning. It was like the farewell speech the day before. There was no artifice or rhetoric. Just a simple statement from the heart revealing how he felt.

My one meeting with Sachin should have made me aware of this many years ago. It did not because I didn't know how to interpret what was so visibly present.

It happened in 1999. I had flown to Bombay to interview Sachin for our BBC programme *Face to Face*. After many weeks of reluctance,

Sachin agreed when Mark Mascarenhas, his agent, recommended he should.

Having decided to do it, Sachin was keen we should meet before the recording to gauge what I was looking for. So, the day before, my producer, Vishal Pant and I went to Sachin's flat in Bandra East. The only other person present was his wife Anjali.

'What sort of answers do you want?' Sachin asked. This was not an interview about cricket but about Sachin himself, a subject he wasn't used to speaking about.

'We've done a lot of research,' I began. 'We've read the cuttings, spoken to your brother, even to Anjali. They've told us about little incidents and anecdotes that together reveal what you're like. So I'm going to ask questions which are actually prompts for you to tell those stories!'

Sachin was silent for a while. I could sense he was thinking about what he'd heard. 'Give me an example of the sort of story you think works.' I did.

This time his response was faster. 'Can you tell me what are the incidents or anecdotes you've chosen so I'm ready and prepared?' And then he smiled in that cherubic way the country has come to love. It's childlike, innocent and beguiling. But he knows how powerful its impact can be.

'You see,' he added, 'I'm not used to this, so I need to be prepared.'

The next day we met at the Oberoi for the recording. Vishal and I were apprehensive but Sachin was full of delightful stories. We intended a twenty minute interview. We ended up with one double that length.

I now realise this was another aspect of Sachin's goodness. He wanted to give his best even in a field where he was, at the time, relatively inexperienced. He didn't want to disappoint and was prepared to put in extra effort.

These days to say someone is a good person is to damn with faint praise. That's a reflection of our cynical time and its twisted values. But to be called good is to be specially valued. I wouldn't use that adjective of too many people. Nor, I suspect, would you!

6

A Rewarding Encounter

He was smiling when he walked through the double doors of the hotel. It was a shy smile. Although he is tall and well built, it made him look young and vulnerable. His appearance and manner suggested informality and friendliness.

My mind raced back to the time when I first met him. This is exactly how he looked when we first met in 1994. Then he was just Viswanathan Anand. When I met him again in 2001, he was the World Chess Champion. Earlier he had come alone. This time his wife, Aruna, was with him. But that apart nothing else had changed.

'Hi,' I said as I stepped forward to greet him.

'We've met before,' he replied, his smile broadening.

'Do you remember?' I asked, surprised that he should.

'Of course,' he said, 'I even remember the prediction I made.'

That shook me. In 1994, the young Anand had claimed he would be world chess champion in two years' time. His first attempt was in 1995 when he lost to Kasparov by a margin of three games. His next shot was three years later and on that occasion he lost to Karpov in a spine-tingling tiebreaker. Although on Christmas Eve in 2000, he fulfilled his ambition, I assumed he would want to forget his earlier rash claim. I was wrong.

'Yeah,' he said, continuing the conversation, 'I'm a few years late but I did it nevertheless.'

I was soon to realise that Anand has the strength to say what he feels and the character to stand by it. In an age when the rest of us take recourse in political correctness, Anand's candour is refreshing. It also wins respect and admiration.

The first example happened almost by accident. We were sitting in the bar of the Chola Sheraton except it had been emptied of all other guests and we were the only ones. In five minutes we were going to start recording the interview Anand had come to give. This was a pause to catch one's breath before the lights were switched on and the cameras started to roll.

'I had no idea the weather in Madras would be so pleasant,' I said and then, realising my error, hastily added, 'sorry, I mean Chennai.'

'Don't worry, I say Madras all the time,' Anand quickly reassured me. 'You know for twenty-eight years of my life, it's been Madras. That's how I think of it. Just because they've changed the name for political reasons doesn't mean I am going to change the way I think of my home city.'

He was right. If in English, Paris is Paris and not *Paree*, if Rome is Rome and not *Roma* and Delhi is Delhi and not *Dilli* or *Dehlee*, then why can't Madras continue as Madras? Or Bombay as Bombay? And Calcutta as Calcutta? Call them what you want in Tamil or Marathi or Bengali but let them stay unchanged in English. After all, Germany is Germany and not Deutschland and the Germans don't object. In fact, when speaking English, Germans themselves call it Germany.

The second example was, if anything, even more revealing. The interview over, Anand was asked by the crew if they could have photographs taken with him. There were fifteen of them and each wanted a personal photograph. Anand had to pose individually in each case. Most of our other star guests grimace when similar requests are made and their reluctance is writ large on their face.

'I'm sorry,' I said gently, trying to ease Anand into agreeing. 'You seem to be very popular.'

'Oh, don't worry,' he answered, at once aware of what I was doing. 'Don't worry' is a favourite phrase. 'After all, where would I be if people did not want autographs and photographs?'

Several of Bollywood's bright and best would do well to take heed of Anand's words. It would be indiscreet, even invidious, for me to name them. My colleagues and crew, however, would have no such compunction.

'You know Anand,' I said, as we chatted after the interview, 'you're so different to the image the world has of you.'

The après-interview—a bit like the après-ski—is a time to let one's hair down and relax. Even the most taciturn of interviewees can become garrulous. I suppose it's partly to do with a sense of relief that the ordeal is over and partly the realisation that Karan is not the rakshasa most people anticipate. In Anand's case, my comment was provoked by the fact that he seemed relaxed and chatty from the start. He's one of the easiest people to talk to.

'And what is this image the world has of me?'

'Strong, silent, dominating and taciturn,' I replied. I thought I had summed it up rather neatly.

'God how wrong that is!'

It wasn't Anand speaking. It was Aruna. 'He's not like that at all. He's the chattiest person I know.'

I noticed Anand was laughing. His eyes were lit up and twinkling with mischief. How little we know him, I thought.

'I find it very hard to be serious when I'm not playing,' he said still chortling. 'I can't be focused and dedicated all the time. In fact, sometimes I find it hard to be focused even when I'm playing!'

'You know,' Aruna added, 'when we first got married he used to say I was a gossip. Now I know he's the biggest chatterbox there is!'

Anand filled all the awkward gaps and pauses with cheerful banter. Not for a moment did I or my colleagues feel we were in the company of a world chess champion. From the start he had us at our ease.

'*Kamal ka aadmi hei,*' said Nirmal, the director, once Anand had left. '*Itne* successful *lekin itne* simple.'

True. How little we know the good and great and yet, how easily we form the wrong impression of them. A few, like Anand, are much, much nicer than we think.

7

Leander Paes

Sometimes the questions you don't ask turn out to be the most important. On such occasions, all you can do is kick yourself. Well, I'm black and blue.

I interviewed Leander Paes in February 2001. He had achieved so much in his twenty-seven years that it was hard to know where to start and impossible to decide what to leave out. There were the four Grand Slam doubles finals, the two titles, the Wimbledon mixed doubles championship, the triumphs as a junior at the US Open and the near misses in Australia, the Davis Cup victories for India, the incredible feats against the likes of Pete Sampras, Goran Ivanišević and Henri Leconte and, of course, there was the Olympic medal. And then there was the rest of his life including his troubles with Bhupathi.

So, in this profusion, a small little question I had worked out about a missing link when he was sixteen got forgotten. In 1990, the young Leander was the losing finalist at the Australian junior Grand Slam, the winner of the Wimbledon junior and he needed only one point to end the year as the world's top junior player. No Indian has ever achieved this distinction. All that was required for Leander to do so was participate in the US Open junior championship. Even a straight sets defeat in the opening round would have been sufficient. But he didn't play. Why? Having failed to ask during the interview—there was so much else to talk about you wouldn't have missed it till you read this confession—I decided to pop the question over coffee afterwards.

Leander laughed but there was pain in his laughter. The memory I had rekindled still hurt. His normally smiling face grew tense, his eyes became serious, his voice grave.

'The Amritrajs wouldn't let me,' he began. 'At the time I was at their tennis academy in Madras and at the very last minute they changed their mind. The flights were confirmed, the hotels booked, my bags packed. In fact, I was leaving that evening when they cancelled everything.'

'But why?' I asked, perplexed by this explanation.

'Jealousy,' he said without hesitation. 'I'm pretty blunt and outspoken. If I had ended the year as the world junior number one, I would have bettered their record and they weren't going to have that.'

So the honour went to an Italian. Worse, someone Leander had repeatedly beaten. No doubt the next year he won the US Open junior championship but the distinction of being the first and the only Indian to end the year as junior number one eluded him.

'Damn,' I said not caring for my language. 'I meant to ask you this during the interview but there was so much else to talk about it got left out. Would you have been equally frank if I had?'

'Maybe I would have expressed myself more delicately,' he said, smiling for the first time. 'But, in the end, I am sure you would have got it out of me!'

Not much consolation in that, I'm afraid.

8

Not Quite Cricket

The truth is I don't understand cricket and don't particularly like it either. To me, it's just elaborate *gulli danda*. Though I watch when I have no alternative, I could just as easily switch off. More often than not, I do. Frankly, cricket bores me.

Mummy, who's nearly ninety-five, finds my attitude inexplicable and unforgiveable. She's a cricket fanatic and often reminisces about her days at the pitch. She claims she was a nifty bowler. My dismissive comments rile her even when I'm clearly teasing. 'Stop it at once,' she admonishes. 'You don't realise how stupid that sounds!' In her cricket-crazy eyes, her son's indifference is a terrible failing.

Perhaps, but the game is my Achilles heel. It brings out the worst in me. On the one occasion I can remember playing—Juniors 3 at Doon School—a lofted catch came sailing through the sky straight to me. I stared at the descending ball whilst cries of 'catch it' rent the air.

Unfortunately, when you look up you also look straight at the sun and the wretched thing is blinding. The ball plopped into my outstretched hands but as I blinked to avoid the glare, I failed to retain it. The ball fell to the ground and continued its journey to the boundary. I was replaced at a hastily taken drinks break.

This should have ended my hapless association with the game but fate had more misfortune in store. In 1974, whilst at Stowe, India toured England. The game that followed had the whole school riveted. India began reasonably enough scoring 302 all out. But England were devastating. They posted 629.

Everyone could sense an English victory except me, of course. Misplaced patriotism made me boast we were going to win. To prove my point, I placed myself bang in front of the box in the common room.

Guess what? India crashed out for 42 runs in 17 overs. It was over before lunch. The next day's papers said it was India's worst ever test score. Alas, no one let me forget it. For the rest of the term, every sod I met began with the question, 'What's the score, Karan?'

Years later, when I began interviewing for the BBC, an early guest was Rahul Dravid. This thrilled my colleagues. It filled me with dread. I knew something would go wrong. I wasn't mistaken.

It was 1999 and I was a novice. So I researched intensely, consulted widely, wrote careful questions, learnt them by heart and rehearsed laboriously. Then the interview began.

Rahul had just returned from the World Cup in England. That's also where he played his first match. As the mikes were fixed he told me how fond he was of the country. Recklessly casting my careful preparation aside, that's how I started.

'It must have been galling to miss a century in your first test by just five wickets?' Rahul stared at me in befuddled silence. I smiled expectantly. Then he threw his head back and laughed uproariously. He was generous enough not to correct me and I only realised what I had said when the interview was broadcast.

And then I tried my luck again. India's collapse at English hands was the subject of a prime-time discussion. 'The problem was the moving ball,' pronounced Tiger Pataudi. 'What?' I said to myself, 'I thought that's what the ball is meant to do?' But sensing danger I bit my lips and kept silent. For once I got away unscathed!

9

Did You Know?

I had just finished a series of interviews for the BBC with India's young cricket stars in May 2004 and I was fascinated by the little details I'd discovered. The young men were, of course, thirteen separate individuals, yet, their lives had common bonds that suggested a leitmotif or, at least, a hint of significance; a little seamless web whose silken threads weave a pattern that must have been accident but felt uncannily like design.

For instance, whilst you might have known that Irfan Pathan's father is the muezzin at the Jama Masjid at Vadodara and that as a child, Irfan would often help sweep the mosque and, occasionally, call the *azaan*, were you aware that at least four of his colleagues come from similar backgrounds? Sanjay Bangar's grandparents were agricultural daily wage labourers. In fact, his father left home because they couldn't afford to educate him. Mohammad Kaif's father is a ticket inspector on the Allahabad–Prayagraj Express. Zaheer Khan's father is a small-town photographer at Srirampur in Maharashtra. Romesh Powar's was a compounder.

Could it be denied that their determination and unflinching spirit was in part a product of their struggle? They weren't to the manor born. Instead, they kicked down the front door to enter. That's why they're so different to the Pataudis, Gavaskars, Tendulkars or Gangulys we're accustomed to.

The similarities, however, go further. Though only in their twenties then, many had experienced the trauma of being dropped and the struggle to get back into the team: Lakshmipathy Balaji was dropped immediately after his debut; Hemang Badani was dropped six months later; Yuvraj within his first year. Murali Kartik (whose real name is Kartik Murali) was dropped eight times in four years! But none succumbed to these setbacks. Faced with adversity, they were defiant. Balaji bowled six consecutive five-wicket Ranji scores. Badani made 127 against New Zealand despite a fractured hand. Kartik kept trying even if he kept getting dropped as well.

Whilst it's the grit and spirit they have in common that's their real link, fate also seems to have dealt them similar hands. No one can forget Ashish Nehra's last over in Karachi. Pakistan needed nine runs off six balls. It came down to six off the last ball but Nehra's bowling ensured that was too much. What you may not remember is that two months earlier, in January in Adelaide, Sanjay Bangar faced an identical situation. Australia needed nine off the last over. Ganguly threw the ball to Bangar, a choice that was as surprising as Nehra in Karachi. Bangar conceded a couple of runs and got a wicket. But, once again, it came down to six off the last ball. Dion Ebrahim, like Moin Khan, skied the shot. The stadium held its breath but it failed to reach the boundary. India won.

Often the coincidences signify nothing but they're still striking. When Kaif scored his famous 87 to clinch victory in the NatWest Trophy, his parents missed seeing their son's triumph. When Irfan Pathan got his first wicket (Matthew Hayden at Adelaide), his parents did not possess a television set to see it. Parthiv Patel's career has been guided by his father's brother, Jagatbhai; Irfan's by his mother's brother, Ahmed Mian. When he was three, Zaheer was almost electrocuted. He was playing with live electricity wires. Irfan was two when he fell into a well. He lay there unconscious until passers-by came to his rescue.

Intriguingly, the coincidences continue off the field. Kartik proposed to his wife Shweta at 5.30 am in the morning. She was in Singapore, he in Delhi. Kartik would not put the phone down till Shweta said yes. Sulakshna kept Hemang on tenterhooks for four years. Their only contact was the phone. Sulakshna foiled all Hemang's attempts to meet her. And when he proposed, she thought it was a joke!

But what I personally find most admirable is that these young cricketers do not fight shy of religion. At their age, I found it difficult to handle the subject. Not them. Balaji, Irfan, Zaheer, Sanjay Bangar, Aakash Chopra and Ramesh Powar speak about their belief with a certainty and an assurance I did not possess.

Are these just coincidences? Perhaps they are. But isn't it uncanny that the new generation of Indian cricketers should have so many striking similarities? No doubt it's their talent that makes them special. But behind their individual skill is the small but significant way fate has fashioned them from the same mould. Could this be the hand of destiny?

10

Katrina Kaif

It may come as a surprise but talking about yourself is not as easy as you might think. No doubt all of us can natter to our friends or family and we're never short of things to say. But I'm talking of a formal interview where you are the subject of the discussion. That's when it can be difficult to be either convincing or charming.

The problem is not simply one of nerves. Nor is it merely an outcome of the environment in which the interview is concluded. Of course these things matter but I'm referring to a bigger problem. How does one present oneself to a stranger in a way that is positive but also truthful, candid but without giving away secrets and yet, engaging and revealing and still not breach your privacy?

I feel it's a knack some people have but many do not. No doubt you can be taught how to attempt to do it and a few succeed. But even at their best, they sound or look tutored. Only a few are naturals. They do it without thinking or even trying. When they speak about themselves, you not only feel you've understood them but come to like and even admire them.

Katrina Kaif is one such person. She was my guest at the India Today Conclave and everyone was riveted not only by the natural and winning aplomb, honesty and charm but also the reserve and carefulness with which she answered my questions.

When I questioned her about Salman Khan, Ranbir Kapoor and Deepika Padukone, Katrina did not seem to hold back, shy away or evade. The words just flowed out of her mouth. But she wasn't always answering the question or, at least, carefully not revealing what I had tried to pry. On occasion, she had sound and eloquent reasons for not doing so. On others, she said as much as she was happy to before leading me to another, but equally absorbing, aspect of the subject.

On some occasions, Katrina actually used the truth as a charming foil to stop a second question. Here's an example: 'When *Vogue* magazine asked you what you would want to be if you weren't an actress, what made you say "Lord Protector of England"?' Her answer was short, simple and truthful. 'I wasn't being serious,' but then she added, 'you have to admit it's a gorgeous sounding job!' Not just me, Oliver Cromwell would also agree!

The overall impression Katrina created was that she always answered my questions and, because at times hers were long answers, she had also covered them fully. But often the truth was different. There were occasions when beguilingly, yet always intelligently and never defensively, she sidestepped several issues. This is a trick politicians need to learn. When they evade, they do it so obviously they're always caught out!

Now, I won't deny that a beautiful woman has a huge advantage convincing the audience she's adequately answered the question she's been asked. But looks cannot provide cover for long. A discerning audience wants more. Katrina intuitively sensed that and her answers to awkward, or even intrusive, questions reflected her instinct not to smile and simply evade but find a way of answering without revealing secrets she wished to protect. She was constantly thinking and well aware of the image she was crafting for herself.

Bravo Katrina!

'Delights' Of English Language

1

English Richness

Is English the richest of all languages? Not being fluent in any other, I have no way of answering that question authoritatively. But that said and done, I suspect the answer could be yes. So, purely on the basis of a crude hunch, let me explain why.

First, the English tradition of separate and unique collective nouns for a variety of wildlife. I admit I'm fascinated by this. Most of us know of shoals of fish, packs of wolves, flocks of geese, herds of elephants or prides of lions. But here are a few that took me completely by surprise. The credit goes to Bambi Rao and Syeda Imam who sent out a round-robin email. For instance, did you know of a pod of whales, a rafter of turkeys, a muster of peacocks, a coffle of asses (when roped together), a drove of asses (when driven), a skein of geese (when in flight) and a skulk of foxes?

Not to be outdone by his own discoveries, Bambi has also suggested a collective noun for bankers. Borrowing from the good Dr Spooner, he proposes 'a wunch of bankers'!

But it's not just the collective nouns that seem to differ for each animal in English. So does the word for the sounds they make. Dogs bark, cats mew, snakes hiss, wolves howl, horses neigh, tigers roar, cows moo, hyenas laugh, elephants trumpet, mice squeal, pigs grunt, donkeys bray and ducks quack! Can any other language beat that?

Even the statement that birds tweet or chirp can be further refined depending on which birds you have in mind. Crows caw, peacocks scream, owls hoot, swallows titter, parrots squawk, doves coo, nightingales warble, magpies chatter, cocks crow, turkeys gobble whilst larks, believe it or not, sing!

Now, you could ask why the English language has such well-defined specificity for wildlife and indeed, birds in particular. The answer, I suspect, may have something to do with nineteenth-century mid-Victorian zoology and ornithology. Or just plain British eccentricity. Either way, it has made the language delightful and wondrous.

However, it's not just the fact that the English language has specific collective nouns for different collections of wildlife or precise terms for the sounds they produce that could make it the richest of all; it also has a variety of different synonyms for the same word. According to *The Oxford English Thesaurus*, there are 380 for the simple word 'good'. And, if you believe what you read on the net, a certain Paul Dickson of the United States has found more than 3,000 for the word 'drunken'. They're all included in a book called *Drink: The Definitive Drinker's Dictionary*! And I would add that if you lay your hands on a good thesaurus, you could while away several hours in amused wonderment.

The sad part is that this rich heritage has not just fallen into disuse but is in danger of being forgotten except by the fussy or the aged. After all, how often do we use the 'right' collective noun or the mot juste for a particular sound? Rarely, if ever, is the answer. Worse, those who do are often sniggered at.

Instead of rejoicing in the richness English offers, we've all dumbed down and happily settled for the limited range of sms-speak. Imprecise words like 'good', 'nice', 'bad' and the dreadful 'awesome' have colonised our minds and begun to dominate our speech. Quite frankly, the loss is ours.

2

Under a Spelling

Unless I'm mistaken, it was a Hindi teacher at Doon School who first made me aware of the idiosyncrasies of English pronunciation. Mr Chandna was a small man, with a large round head and a very precise way of speaking. When he wanted to make a point, he would do it with a delightful degree of overemphasis.

'What sort of language is this?' he would begin. 'P U T is "put" yet B U T is "but". N O is "no" but K N O W is also "know"! There's no consistency, no rules, no logic. That's just the way it is.'

At the time, I found Mr Chandna's comment witty. An email from my cousin Lakshman Menon who, incidentally, Mr Chandna failed to make proficient in Hindi, has made me realise how profound his witticism actually was.

Read the following paragraph and see if you can get the pronunciation correct without pausing to double-check and reconsider. And here is a tip: If you've got the pronunciation right, the meaning will be obvious. If not, it'll be gobbledygook:

- The bandage was wound around the wound.
- The farm was used to produce produce.
- The dump was so full that it had to refuse more refuse.
- We must polish the Polish furniture.

- He could lead if he would get the lead out.
- The soldier decided to desert his dessert in the desert.
- Since there is no time like the present, he thought it was time to present the present.
- When shot at, the dove dove into the bushes.
- I did not object to the object.
- The insurance was invalid for the invalid.
- There was a row among the oarsmen about how to row.
- They were too close to the door to close it.
- The buck does funny things when the does are present.
- To help with planting, the farmer taught his sow to sow.
- The wind was too strong to wind the sail.
- Upon seeing the tear in the painting, I shed a tear.
- I had to subject the subject to a series of tests.
- How can I intimate this to my most intimate friend?

Most of the above trick words are homonyms. That is to say they are different words, with different meanings but with the same spelling. However, it's even more intriguing—or do I mean confusing?—when the pronunciation is the same but the spelling is different. Beach and Beech are examples. So too witch and which. Or blue and blew. And, if you're a little weary, don't forget tire and tyre!

So, what's the conclusion? Words with different spellings can have the same pronunciation whilst words with the same spelling can have different pronunciations! This also means that just because you know how to speak it, you don't necessary know how to write English or if you can spell it correctly, that's no guarantee you can pronounce it properly.

If it's any consolation, the British don't have an agreed pronunciation for their language. They may call it 'the Queen's English' but her pronunciation is by no means a guide for her subjects. They revel—or rebel?—in regional accents. Henry Higgins makes the point most tellingly in *My Fair Lady*, 'Why can't the English teach their children how to speak? This verbal class distinction by now should be antique!' Alas, he failed. And, as Mr Chandna declared, 'That's just the way it is.'

3

Thank You, Miss Truss

I wonder how often you think of the comma, the colon or the semicolon. Or for that matter the hyphen, the dash and the apostrophe? Normally, punctuation is not something we concern ourselves with. We assume we know it, we certainly don't hesitate to use it but—that said and done—we also don't care about it.

A small, clever and wittily-written book with the intriguing title *Eats, Shoots and Leaves*, which was a runaway success in Britain and topped the Christmas charts in 2003, shows how mistaken is our confidence. I read an extract in the tabloid *Times*, found my curiosity aroused, rushed off to buy the book and couldn't put it down. It didn't take me long to read. I recommend it most highly and if you can't find it in your local bookshop, insist it's ordered as fast as possible.

The point the book makes is simple: The power of punctuation may be unappreciated but it is beyond all doubt. When Victor Hugo wanted to ask his publisher how *Les Misérables* was selling, he telegraphed the simple enquiry '?' and received the succinct but satisfactory answer '!'. Alas, in the 150 years since, we've forgotten how useful these marks of convention can be. Lynne Truss, the author, argues it's all to do with our age's preference for the cryptic telegraphic writing of email and telephone text over proper, grammatical and preferably handwritten prose.

Consider these examples connected with the use of the comma to appreciate her point. The sign 'No dogs please' is commonly seen in most parts of the world. But without the comma it doesn't mean what you think it does, namely, that dogs are not permitted. Instead, it suggests that dogs do not give pleasure or, at any rate, are not pleasing. Here's another example: 'The convict said the judge is mad'. On first reading you could be forgiven for assuming the convict has a low opinion of the judge. But place a comma after convict and another after judge ('The convict, said the judge, is mad') and the sense is virtually reversed.

However, it's not just the absence of a comma that can change meaning. Incorrect placement can be equally devastating. As written, the following sentence is perplexing: 'Shanta walked on her head, a little higher than usual'. But move the comma to come after the word on and the sentence makes instant sense.

Sadly, the comma is not the only punctuation we stumble over. If anything, the apostrophe presents a more formidable hurdle. Let me explain. If Dick had an in tray you could call it Dick's in tray. But omit the apostrophe and it would read Dicks in tray and you might well wonder what they were doing there. Or when, on entering a hotel, you see the sign 'New members welcome drink' you might think you are being offered one but, in fact, all you are being told is the statement that new members welcome drink. No doubt they do. The sign that would legitimately gladden your heart should read 'New member's welcome drink'.

However, when it comes to the apostrophe, it's not a simple choice between using one and not doing so. Most people don't know where to place it. For instance, if you want to criticise a poor quality glass of wine you could call it Frog's Piss but as Lynne Truss points out, that puts an awful lot of strain on a single frog. Frogs' Piss is more appropriate. But Rommie's home is the correct way of referring to his house even if the large-heartedness of the man makes you want to call it Rommies'. Incidentally, I'm told on good authority there's still only one of him!

Permit me one last example; a piece of punctuation we use increasingly but unthinkingly: The ellipsis or, if you prefer, the dot, dot, dot (...) things that appear all over our text messages. How many of us realise that officially it has only two specific functions? To indicate that words are missing from a quoted passage or to trail off in an intriguing fashion. To use it in place of a full stop or dash is not just misleading—at least to those who know what it should mean—but also wasteful of both space and effort.

Now let me return to the title of the book which has, as you've seen, triggered off so many thoughts on a subject I've hardly considered since I left school. *Eats, Shoots and Leaves* is a little joke which aptly illustrates the point Miss Truss wishes to make. This is how it goes:

A panda walks into a cafe. He orders a sandwich, eats it, then draws a gun and fires two shots in the air.

'Why?' asks the waiter, as the panda makes towards the exit. The panda produces a badly punctuated wildlife manual and tosses it over his shoulder.

'I'm a panda,' he says, at the door. 'Look it up.'

The waiter turns to the relevant entry and sure enough, finds an explanation.

'Panda. Large black-and-white bear-like mammal, native to China. Eats, shoots and leaves.'

4

The Joys of English!

There's no doubt English is a rather peculiar language. It's not just the way words are spelt and pronounced that's arbitrary but the rules of grammar and punctuation appear to exist only to be flouted.

We all know that BUT is 'but', though PUT is 'put', yet PUTT sounds just like 'but'. Why the extra 'T' should change the pronunciation of the 'U' is hard to explain. However add an 'O' or 'I'—to make 'putto' or 'putti' and the pronunciation of the 'U' changes once again. Now change the last letter to a 'Y' to make 'putty' and you've reversed the sound of the 'U'!

English grammar and punctuation are riddled with similar inconsistencies. For instance, do you need a comma before an 'and'? Should you write 'a dog, a cat and a horse' or 'a dog, a cat, and a horse'? The answer is both are correct although Lynn Truss, the author of *Eats, Shoots and Leaves*, believes the comma before the 'and'—the Oxford comma, as it's called—is redundant.

Much of this can be great fun. However, what I find most amusing is the origin of the phrases we use every day. For instance, did you know that the expression 'cost you an arm and a leg' lies in eighteenth-century portrait painting? Apparently, at the time the price charged depended on how many limbs were shown in the painting. The more arms and legs in the picture, the more the work involved and the higher the cost. Hence, the phrase it'll 'cost you an arm and a leg'!

The phrase 'minding your Ps and Qs' has an equally interesting story behind it. In the days when beer was served in taverns in pints and quarts, barmaids had to keep a count of and distinguish between customers drinking in pints and those quaffing in quarts. In other words, she had to 'mind her Ps and Qs'!

My favourite, however, is the explanation of the phrase it's 'cold enough to freeze the balls off a brass monkey'. I always thought it was lewd. The truth is quite otherwise. Hard as it may be to believe, the origin stretches back to the heyday of sailing ships. At the time, all ships carried iron canons which fired iron balls. Because it was necessary to keep a good supply of balls near the canon, a way had to be found to do so compactly and without the balls rolling around the deck. The initial answer was to stack them in a pyramid. This ensured they didn't take up too much space but it still left the bottom row free to slide out from underneath. So a metal plate called a monkey was devised with round indentations to fit the balls. And to guard against the plate and balls rusting, it was made of brass. But brass contracts faster and further than iron in cold temperatures. So when the weather turned freezing, the indentations would shrink and the iron balls would come right off the monkey. Thus, it was quite literally, 'cold enough to freeze the balls off a brass monkey'!

Even individual words have intriguing histories. For instance, we all gossip and even those who deny it enjoy doing so. But the origin of the word is at times believed to lie in the need politicians have for feedback from the public. Long before television or radio, politicians would send their assistants to taverns and pubs with the instruction 'go sip some ale' and report on the conversations they heard. What they returned with came to be called 'gossip'.

And guess how important people ended up as 'big wigs'? It goes back to a time when men regularly wore wigs but that's not all. The wealthy wore wigs made of wool which, if washed, would shrink or lose shape.

So, when dirty, they were baked. The inside dough was scraped out of a large loaf of bread, the wig placed in the shell and baked for thirty minutes. The heat would make them large and fluffy. What emerged was literally a big wig. When worn, it was proof the owner was wealthy and powerful.

Finally, do today's chairmen know their designation has a rather literal origin? In the early 1700s, most English homes could only afford a single chair. It was kept for the head of the household though the privilege was often shared with important guests. Consequently, the 'chairman' was a man of significance. Incidentally, women were kept standing!

5

Unbelievable Words

'Triskaidekaphobia!' The look of pain on Pertie's face was unmistakable as he struggled and failed to pronounce this hybrid term. 'What sort of word is that?'

At the best of times, polysyllabic creations defeat Pertie's pronunciation. However, this inelegant Greco-Latin derivation proved particularly difficult. He managed the first syllable, attempted the second and then slurred over the rest. I daresay it's a form of phonophobia which, believe it or not, is fear of sounds or speaking aloud. But since he had obviously read one of my earlier articles, I bit my tongue and didn't say a word. I didn't even smile.

Pertie was reacting to a word I used in a previous article. Triskaidekaphobia is fear of thirteen. Like phonophobia, it's created around the Greek word phobia which means fear. The first syllable defines what sort of fear it is. Today, however, their Greek origin is only interesting etymology. They are now English words and both are examples of the extraordinary richness of that language.

English has or can devise a word for almost everything. Other languages have to devote cumbersome sentences to explain or describe things. In English, there's usually a single, if not always simple, word for it which is why English translations of French or Arabic speakers on television finish long before the person stops talking.

But back to the joys of the English language and my claim that it seems to have a word for everything. For instance, did you know that the *Chambers Twenty-first Century Dictionary* lists fifty-eight different phobias? Look up phobias on the net and the number jumps to an astonishing 530! The single largest collection starts with the letter A (sixty-nine). Close up behind are those beginning with P (sixty-three). Oddly, there are none starting with Q,Y and Z. Each is the precise word for describing a specific condition. Of course, the vast majority is unused, if not also unknown but their existence, as much as the fear they describe, is fascinating.

I knew of agoraphobia (fear of open spaces), claustrophobia (its opposite), homophobia (to do with homosexuals) and xenophobia (foreigners). But who could have guessed there was such a thing as fear of crossing bridges (gephyrophobia) or fear of sharp objects such as knives (aichmophobia) or even fear of the colour red (erythrophobia)?

An aunt of mine has mysophobia (fear of contamination or dirt), most kids before they learn to swim have hydrophobia (water), several adults can't shake off either cynophobia (dogs) or ailurophobia (cats), whilst I'm sure each and every one of us has ophidiophobia (fear of snakes).

Some of the phobias might seem amusing or perplexing unless, of course, you're Indian and can fully understand them. There's fear of work (ponophobia), which affects every Indian office. Or, there's fear of writing (graphophobia) and fear of books (bibliophobia), which lurk in our schools and sometimes even our universities. And, finally, there's fear of people (anthropophobia), which the BJP has caught and is still to recover from.

But not all the 530 listed phobias are exotic or quixotic. Some are as common as the everyday cold. So, although you may not know the word, pause and consider how effective it might be to use some of these terms. For example, the next time you try and cross a road in South Extension or Connaught Place, and the traffic keeps rushing past, remember that the panic you feel is simply dromophobia. Or if you're the sort who jumps at the slightest sound in the dark there's a word for it—scotophobia. Nyctophobia seems to be another. And if spiders make you crawl up the wall or at least, scream and rush out of the loo you've got arachnophobia.

These are delightful words for common symptoms that otherwise we would spend full sentences explaining. Of course the condition they describe is neither serious nor embarrassing. But what do you make of phobophobia (fear of fearing)? Or pantophobia (fear of everything)? The only thing worse is to develop androphobia or gynophobia on your wedding night. That's fear of men or women. Of course, erotophobia could be understandable as long as the condition doesn't persist. Given our population problem I doubt if it will!

And if Pertie's reading this article, I'd like to tell him he has haemophobia (fear of blood) and algophobia (pain), which is a polite way of saying he's a coward. Meanwhile, my favourite is Hippopotomonstrosesquippedaliophobia. Quite appropriately, it means fear of long words. But alas, I don't know how to pronounce it!

One question remains: Why am I so fascinated by words? After all, language is full of them and, as Humpty Dumpty said in *Alice in Wonderland*, 'I use words to mean what I want them to mean!' So what's so special about them? They can be malleable, idiosyncratic, confusing or even misleading. But the funny thing is that is their charm. Because words are powerful. Like weapons or as Atal Bihari Vajpayee once said like arrows that you shoot from the mouth—once spoken they can't be recalled and they become public property. After that you can quarrel over their meaning.

The truth is that words are powerful. Perhaps more so than anything else. As children we would argue whether the pen is mightier than the sword. Of course it is. But only because it writes words. When the pen writes gibberish, the sword wins any day. But when well-chosen words flow from its nib, the flow of ink is infinitely more lasting and more impressive than the slash of a sword.

So perhaps the worst of all phobias is verbophobia. That, as you must have guessed, is fear of words!

'Daylights' Of English Language

1 English, as She's Spoken and Written

Sixty-eight years after Independence when we snapped our links with the British Raj, spare a thought for the complexities of the language we've continued with and steadily, if not proudly, mangled and mispronounced. But to be honest, the blame is not ours. It lies squarely with the English language. There isn't another that lends itself so deliciously to misspelling and faulty pronunciation.

First, consider this popular email I received from my friend Vishakh Rathi. The point it makes should be obvious:

> The European Commission has just announced an agreement whereby English will be the official language of the European Union rather than German, which was the other possibility. As part of the negotiations, the British government conceded that English spelling had some room for improvement and has accepted a five-year phase-in plan that would become known as 'Euro-English'.
>
> In the first year, 's' will replace the soft 'c'. Sertainly, this will make the sivil servants jump with joy. The hard 'c' will then be dropped in favour of 'k'. This should klear up konfusion and keyboards kan have one less letter.
>
> There will be growing publik enthusiasm in the sekond year when the troublesome 'ph' will be replaced with 'f'. This will make words like fotograf 20 per cent shorter.

In the third year, publik akseptanse of the new spelling kan be expekted to reach the stage where more komplikated changes are possible. Governments will enkourage the removal of double letters which have always ben a deterrent to akurate speling. Also, al wil agre that the horibl mes of the silent 'e' in the languag is disgrasful and it should go away. By the fourth yer, people wil be reseptiv to steps such as replasing 'th' with 'z' and 'w' with 'v'.

During ze fifz yer, ze unesesary 'o' kan be dropd from vords kontaining 'ou' and after ziz fifz yer, ve vil hav a reil sensibl riten styl. Zer vil be no mor trubl or difikultis and evrivun vil find it ezi tu understand ech oza. Ze drem of a united urop vil finali kum tru.

Und efter ze fifz yer, ve vil al be speking German like zey vunted in ze forst plas.

If Vishakh's email is about spelling, the following poem which I received from Kris Srinivasan, is about the horrors of pronunciation, particularly when the spelling seems to suggest otherwise. Incidentally, this is one way of discovering whether you really know how to speak the language or only to read and write it. But first, a word of advice—read this poem slowly and carefully because otherwise you're bound to trip up. And mind your tongue!

Brush up Your English

I take it you already know
Of tough and bough and cough and dough.
Others may stumble but not you,
On hiccough, through, lough and though.
Well done! And now you wish, perhaps,
To learn of less familiar traps.

Beware of heard, a dreadful word
That looks like beard and sounds like bird,
And dead—it's said like bed, not bead.
For goodness's sake, don't call it deed!
Watch out for meat and great and threat:
They rhyme with suite and straight and debt.

A moth is not a moth in mother,
Nor both in bother, broth in brother,
And here is not a match for there,
Nor dear and fear for bear and pear,
And then there's dose and rose and lose—
Just look them up—and goose and choose,
And cork and work and card and ward,
And font and front and word and sword,
And do and go and thwart and cart.
Come, come, I've hardly made a start.
A dreadful language? Man alive,
I'd mastered it when I was five.

Finally, in case you're interested, this poem is considered to owe its origin to a certain Gerald Nolst Treniti, a Dutch observer of the English language who lived from 1870 to 1946 and wrote under the pseudonym Charivarius. Perhaps that's also the origin of the expression, 'It's double Dutch'!

2

The Fun of Being Wrong

Have you heard the phrase 'a little knowledge is a dangerous thing?' Well, a little English can lead to a hilarious situation. People, unfamiliar with the language, often express themselves in strange ways. Their intended meaning may be clear but what they've actually said is deliciously and delightfully different. Kris Srinivasan, a connoisseur of such stuff, has sent me an email that had me in splits. Let me share it with you.

It seems hotel notices often get their English wrong. For instance, a bar in Tokyo claims: 'Special cocktails for the ladies with nuts.' On its executive floor, the hotel proclaims: 'You are invited to take advantage of the chambermaid.' But it's not just Asiatics who can't handle the complexities of the Anglo-Saxon tongue. Consider this notice in the lobby of a Moscow hotel: 'You are welcome to visit the cemetery where famous Russian and Soviet composers, artists and writers are buried daily except Thursday.' Unfortunately, the Swiss are no better. This was found in a hotel in Zurich: 'Because of the impropriety of entertaining guests of the opposite sex in the bedroom, it is suggested that the lobby be used for this purpose.'

I thought the Scandinavians knew English well but this sign from a cocktail lounge in Norway suggests otherwise: 'Ladies are requested not to have children in the bar.' However, the English doesn't improve as you head south. The Budapest Zoo states: 'Please do not feed the animals—if you have any suitable food, give it to the guard on duty.' In Rome, a doctor's office states: 'Specialist in women and other diseases.' A nearby laundry advertises itself as follows: 'Ladies, leave your clothes here and spend the afternoon having a good time.'

Oddly enough, former British colonies fare no better. If you thought British rule ensured a good grasp of English, think again. A restaurant in Nairobi says: 'Customers who find our waitresses rude ought to see the manager.' A dentist in Hong Kong maintains: 'Teeth extracted by the latest methodists'. Even in our own dear Bombay, you can find a restaurant which claims: 'Open seven days a week and weekends too.'

My favourites come from two countries where there's no reason to expect fluency in English. A tourist agency in Czechoslovakia offers its services with the following promise: 'Take one of our horse-driven city tours and we guarantee no miscarriages.' And then there's this advertisement for donkey rides in Thailand: 'Would you like to ride on your own ass?'

Now, the only thing that can better a mistake is famous people expressing themselves with a certain twisted pithiness. If the incorrect notices are funny, this is pure wit. Jimmy Carter's mother, Lillian, once said: 'Sometimes, when I look at my children, I say to myself "Lillian, you should have remained a virgin."' Eleanor Roosevelt, FD Roosevelt's wife, is credited with the following: 'I had a rose named after me and I was very flattered. But I was not pleased to read the description in the catalogue: "No good in a bed, but fine against a wall."'

Mark Twain was brilliant at this sort of thing. Try this: 'Last week, I stated this woman was the ugliest I had ever seen. I have since been visited by her sister and now wish to withdraw that statement.' Here's another: 'Be careful about reading health books in case you die of a misprint.'

Not surprisingly, some of the wittiest comments have been made by the Brits themselves. For instance, Winston Churchill once said: 'Don't worry about avoiding temptation; as you grow older, it will avoid you.' WC Fields: 'I never drink water because of the disgusting things fish do in it.' Spike Milligan: 'Money can't buy you happiness but it does bring you a more pleasant form of misery.' And, finally, Groucho Marx: 'I was married by a judge. I should have asked for a jury.' This time my favourites are the ones that take something out of context and change its meaning. For instance, Victor Borge: 'Santa Claus has the right idea. Visit people only once a year'. Or Socrates: 'By all means marry. If you get a good wife, you'll become happy; if you get a bad one, you'll become a philosopher.' And Joe Namath: 'Until I was thirteen, I thought my name was SHUT UP'.

Oh well, have a great Sunday.

3

The Words We Use

There's something to be said for Humpty Dumpty. 'When I use a word,' he declared in a rather scornful tone, 'it means just what I choose it to mean, neither more nor less.' And if you think Lewis Carol was cocking a snook at the rest of us, then go back a century to Sheridan and you'll find one of his favourite characters, Mrs Malaprop, claiming a similar right albeit with less authority. Her flair for using words which sound impressive but are, in fact, singularly inept and inappropriate, was so pronounced—and so enjoyable!—the term malapropism was coined to honour her.

I've come to the conclusion that Indian newspapers and magazines exist somewhere between Mrs Malaprop and Humpty Dumpty. They either don't care if the word they're using exists or they use it in such a manner as to invest it with fresh meaning altogether. The result can be hilarious.

'Sex,' pronounced one of our grand editors the other day, 'is a touchy subject.' No doubt it is, but I don't think he intended what he actually said. Mrs Malaprop would have called it 'a nice derangement of epitaphs.' A few pages on, his magazine of which I'm a great fan, presented the results of a weighty survey on the sexual habits of the Indian woman. One of the headlines spread across two pages read: 'Chennai is the most conservative, Delhi, the most experimentative.' Hurray for the capital except there's no such word!

A few years ago, a leading newspaper for whose sister television concern I once worked, made a similarly glorious blunder. It was on the front page. Announcing Morarji Desai's death, the cover story began: 'Yesterday Morarji Desai, aged ninety-nine, died a few months after his 100th birthday.' That could only have happened if he had travelled backwards in time!

Even our stentorian columnists, who roar from exalted platforms, can lapse into linguistic folly. Commenting on a possible resolution the UN Security Council might pass, one of them claimed it would cede a large part of Iraq's control to the United Nations. But, he added in the next sentence, this was too little too late. However, did he realise he was describing an impossible situation? If less had been ceded earlier would that have been sufficient? Or if more was on offer now would that compensate for the delay? And if all he meant was that a lot more was needed a long time ago, then why did he not say so? The cliché 'too little too late' gave his argument the appearance of a well-thought-out dismissal when, in fact, it simply did not make sense.

Sometimes, sadly, the problem goes deeper. You often encounter sentences where individual words are perfectly understandable but together become mind-boggling. Here's an example: 'She is the overconscious perfectionist who turns the imperfections of the stranded traveller into small, beautiful, pleasantly intriguing, set pieces.'

Here, I suspect, words have been used to impress rather than express. And when that happens, you can bet something else is happening as well. The language used is either obscuring the meaning or, more likely, thinly disguising the fact the author is not sure what he wants to say. If he was, he would say it clearly, simply and it would be easy to comprehend.

These are lessons I learnt the hard way. In 1976, in Cambridge, I wrote an essay on Hegel and Marx. I considered it a fine effort. So I awaited my tutor's response with eager anticipation. When it came, I was initially elated.

'This essay,' he scribbled in the margin, 'is well written in a purely literary sense.' But as I reflected on this solitary sentence, I realised it wasn't a compliment. My essay had been found wanting even if my language was pleasing. Thoughts and arguments—which are necessary ingredients—were lacking.

So, let me rest my case on two points. There's nothing so difficult it cannot be said simply. That's an axiom most of us forget most of the time. Equally importantly—and, particularly, if you use words with cleverness and resonance—there's nothing so simple you can't dress it up to look grand. But shorn off ornamental language, it remains an unpolished stone.

I daresay there are also two ways to respond. The first, to borrow a phrase from the good Reverend Spooner, would be to dismiss this as the ranting of 'a shining wit'. If you did, I would wince but accept the blow. The other is to recall that Wittgenstein inaugurated the study of linguistic philosophy with a simple tantalising question 'What is the meaning of a word?' If you don't know or don't care but still insist on using it, are you surprised the rest of us are perplexed by what you are saying?

4

Use of English Language

It's time to once again poke a little fun at the English language or more accurately, our use of it. So if you've had your fill of Anna, inflation, petrol prices and the 2G accused, this is very possibly the remedy you need. Sit comfortably and read on for a little frivolous pleasure.

First, consider how the English language has changed. When I was ten, rubber meant eraser, ass meant donkey, gay meant happy, straight was linear, cock was a rooster, pussy a cat, a prick was a jab, a poke a nudge and a screw was what a carpenter used. Oh yes, in case I forget, a tit was a response for a tat. Now, today, even if you're gay you may prefer not to openly admit it whilst many more are pricks and don't know it. And very few use a rubber! We prefer to use pens or type.

Now, here's an apocryphal account of what the Irish have done to the language. My cousin Arjun claims the *Irish Medical Dictionary* has the following unique definitions for words you and I have always understood differently.

- Bacteria is defined as 'the back door to the cafeteria'
- Caesarian Section as 'a neighbourhood in Rome'
- Cat Scan as 'searching for Kitty'
- Coma as 'a punctuation mark' whilst
- Dilate is 'to live long'

- Enema is 'Not a friend'
- Fester is 'quicker than someone else'
- Fibula 'a small lie'
- Labour Pain 'getting hurt at work'
- Morbid 'a higher offer'
- Nitrates are 'rates of pay for night work'
- Tablet is 'a small table'
- Pelvis is 'a second cousin of Elvis'
- Secretion is 'to hide something'
- Urine is the 'opposite of you're out'
- Terminal Illness is 'getting sick at the airport'

However, more than the Irish, when it comes to destroying the English language, the real offenders are the Americans. Even though Professor Higgins insists they haven't spoken it for years, they've mastered the art of making simple English needlessly complicated. So when an American goes shopping, rather than buy he asks, 'Can I get…?' When he contemplates, rather than choose the easiest he opts for the 'least bad option'. When he arrives, he doesn't disembark but 'deplanes'. Worse, if something happens often, it's said to be 'oftentimes'. And, of course, twice and thrice have been replaced by 'two times' and 'three times'.

Finally, here are the Indianisms—our own unique national contribution to the misery of English—that I once threatened to bombard you with. This is a collection sent by Bambi Rao, to whom I'm, of course, indebted.

Whilst the rest of the world, on finishing their studies, graduate, we 'pass out'. Given our grades perhaps that's more accurate. When we want to ask for a reply, we command 'kindly revert', unaware that it means return to a former state. When we want someone to do something, we state 'kindly do the needful', which presumes they share our need. And famously, when we're away we say we're 'out of station'. I wonder what's wrong with out of town or even, I'm not here?

However, there is one Indianism that serves a most useful purpose and I do recommend it to the English. It's to 'prepone', the opposite of postpone, that is, to bring forward an appointment or an event. Quite frankly, this is a word that we need and it makes a lot of sense. It deserves to exist. So my advice to the lexicographers of the *Oxford English Dictionary* is simple: 'Kindly adjust!'[1]

[1] Editor's note: Happily, the word 'prepone' now appears in the *Oxford English Dictionary*.

5

What an Idea, Sirjee!

Have you noticed how acceptable and widely used English has become? Even when people are speaking Hindi, English words keep popping up. I'm sure this is equally true of conversations in Bengali, Tamil, Telugu, Assamese or Kashmiri. In contrast, Hindi purists seem to have faded away. There was a time when the Mulayam Singh Yadavs were sticklers for '*klisht* Hindi'; now I can't remember when he last objected to the use of English.

My case, however, is established by simply listening to how people speak and pausing to think about the words they use. Consider a few examples. No one—not your mates, nor the *sabji-wallah* or the taxi driver—reels off their mobile number in Hindi. People may still say *ikees*, *arsath* or *ninyanbe* but a mobile number is always spelt out in English, regardless of how misleading the pronunciation may be! Actually, that's also true of ordinary phone numbers.

Better still, eavesdrop on conversations and notice how frequently English words crop up. Here's a selection of sentences I've heard recently: '*Aap ke liye* message *hei*', '*Woh hamesha* late *aatein hein*', '*Mujhe* medicine *leni hei*', '*Phir kaam pe* no-show *hoge*', '*Meri* salary *bahut kum hei*', 'Promotion *nahin mila*', '*Mujhe* loan *chahiye*', 'Black *aap ko bahut* suit *karta hei*', '*Uski* baby girl *hui hei*'. In each case, the English words were used deliberately but they sounded natural. That's because they seem to fit in, they feel as if they belong.

Is this anglicisation? No, it's Englishification. Although that's a pretty dreadful word, what it points towards is three important and, I suspect, irreversible facts. First, an increasing number of people are deliberately using English words either because they are better suited to what they want to say or more impressive. Second, modern lifestyles encourage people to use modern speech, which simultaneously sounds casual, cool and cosmopolitan. And English fits the bill. Third, English—or at any rate English words—is both the link between different Indians and paradoxically, the distinction between our use of English and that of the English-speaking world. It cuts both ways.

However, I would go a step further. The ever-multiplying reliance and acceptability of English shows that we have become comfortable with ourselves and our unique history and circumstances. The colonial hangover which led an earlier generation to protest against English is past and forgotten. We've internalised the language. It's no longer *phoren*, it's become Indian. Second, we're now sure of our identity. Borrowed phrases or concepts don't undermine it. In fact, we often prefer foreign words to express ourselves. And third, being Indian is an umbrella concept, an omnibus idea; it embraces many, often contradictory, qualities and we've become well-adjusted to and increasingly happy with that.

Well, what do you say about all this? My answer is 'What an idea, Sirjee!'

The 'Literary' Affairs

1

Eternal Vigilance is the Price We Pay for Our Liberties

Forty years is not a long time to forget the most traumatic experience of our post-Independence history. But, arguably, that's true of the Emergency. Declared just before midnight on 25 June 1975, today it's not even a memory for the majority of our countrymen. But even for those who still vividly remember it, the experience belongs to history, a past that's well and truly behind us. Or so we hope!

This is why Coomi Kapoor's book *The Emergency: A Personal History* is both so necessary and also such an evocative reminder. Combining a well-researched chronological historical account with personal anecdotal experiences of the impact on individual lives, her book recreates the twenty-one months of the Emergency and what it was like to live in India at that time. For the majority of you, who were born after it ended as well as those of us who were present at the time but have chosen to forget, it's a poignant—and dare I say, opportune?—awakening.

The cold facts of the Emergency are chilling: 34,988 people were detained under the Maintenance of Internal Security Act (MISA) whilst 75,818 were held under the Defence of India rules; virtually the entire Opposition leadership was arrested; the press censored; the Constitution brutally amended and even the Supreme Court accepted that the Right to Life had been suspended. The idea of India was forgotten. Or maybe, it was no longer relevant.

Forty years later, there are three lessons we need to forever hold on to. First, the Emergency was the response of a desperate Prime Minister struggling to protect her political career after the Allahabad High Court struck down her election and the Supreme Court only granted a conditional stay. The excuses she trotted out in its defence, even at their most accurate, lacked credibility. And if Indira Gandhi could have done this to us, we must always be on our guard in case one of her successors attempts something similar. Remember, the most popular can be the most dangerous. After all, in 1971, who was more beloved than her?

The second lesson is, arguably, more necessary. The Emergency, for all its excesses, was constitutionally imposed. Like Hitler used the Enabling Act in 1933, Indira Gandhi used the provisions of our Constitution to snuff out our liberties. And what this means is a majority in Parliament is as much an opportunity for misuse of power as it is an assurance of smooth and good governance. In the hands of a strong and determined leader, it could go either way.

The third lesson is one that should make you both squirm and smile. When the Emergency was declared, India didn't resist. We simply gave in. Not just politicians, the judiciary and the press but us, the people of India. We buckled under. We may have sighed, we may have cried, we may even have sneaked out of harm's way but we did not fight back.

Yet, when Indira Gandhi gave us the chance to vote we proved we were, ultimately, indomitable. They said the poor only care for *roti, kapda aur makaan* and do not value freedom of speech, habeas corpus and due process. We showed them we want both and we got both. In the end, we restored India's democracy.

I passionately hope history doesn't repeat itself and I personally believe it won't. But, remember, eternal vigilance is the price we pay for our liberties. And the most important is the right to dissent.

2

An 'Accident' that Gave Him the Post, Not the Power

You can't have failed to notice how Sanjaya Baru's biography of Dr Manmohan Singh, *The Accidental Prime Minister*, has created a storm. However, the critical question that hasn't been addressed is: Has the book uncovered the dark hidden secrets of the Manmohan Singh prime ministership or simply acknowledged a reality that was staring us in the face?

Of Dr Singh's prime ministership, Baru concludes: 'Many…believe that in not asserting the authority inherent in his office he…devalued it…his willingness to be pushed around by his party and coalition partners and… to have his decisions publicly challenged by Rahul Gandhi, irretrievably damaged his image.'

This was an inevitable consequence of Dr Singh's belief, 'There cannot be two centres of power…I have to accept that the party president is the centre of power.' He, therefore, deliberately subordinated himself to Sonia Gandhi and made the Prime Minister junior to the Congress president.

This is, of course, a distortion of our Constitution. Article 74 makes the Prime Minister the supreme authority in the country. As such, he is accountable to Parliament. By accepting Sonia Gandhi as more powerful, Dr Singh undermined the Constitution, the prime ministership as well as the concept of accountability.

Yet, the undeniable truth is that the mandate of 2004—you may differ about 2009—was for Sonia Gandhi as Prime Minister. She gifted the post to Dr Singh. This clearly demonstrated she had the power to do so. And that power remained with her. No wonder he accepted 'the Party president is the centre of power'. It was reality.

This is why Pulok Chatterji would 'seek her instructions on important files to be cleared by the PM'. This is why she could offer the finance ministership or choose a national security adviser and principal secretary without consulting the Prime Minister. He was, after all, her appointee.

The surprising thing is that it was done quietly, even unobtrusively and didn't attract attention. Each time Sonia exercised her power she, no doubt, undermined the office of the Prime Minister—and that's true of Rahul Gandhi in later years—but it was done with discretion.

This was one reason their diarchy survived and often succeeded. The other is that Dr Manmohan Singh didn't complain. He swallowed whatever slights were meted out to him. But then, what else could he have done?

You could come to the same conclusion about Dr Singh's response to the corruption scandals that overwhelmed his government. Of this, Baru writes: 'Rather than call him blind, I would say that he sometimes chose to close his eyes…he averted his eyes from corruption.' His conclusion: 'He was himself incorruptible, and also ensured that no one in his immediate family ever did anything wrong but he didn't feel answerable for the misdemeanours of his colleagues and subordinates.' It follows Dr Singh could have acted to either prevent corruption or tackle it but consciously chose not to.

On the other hand, what could he have done? He didn't have the power to remove ministers. That lay with their respective party chiefs. If they stood by their errant colleagues, the Prime Minister could only accept or endanger the government. Averting his eyes was his answer. Once again, he was accepting reality.

The truth lies tucked in the phrase Dr Singh once used to describe himself: 'I'm an accidental Prime Minister'. That accident gave him the post but not the power that goes with it.

3

To Natwar with Love

The only thing more fun than reading a letter you've received is poring over one addressed to someone else. Like forbidden fruit, it tastes sweeter. This is why K Natwar Singh's book, *Yours Sincerely*, is such a pleasure.

It's a collection of epistles from people as varied as Indira Gandhi, EM Forster, Han Suyin, Nadine Gordimer, Kenneth Kaunda and believe it or not, AK Antony. The only problem is in most cases, Natwar has forgotten to publish what he wrote to them. I guess it never occurred to him to keep copies of his own! Even if this makes the correspondence a trifle one-sided, it still reveals delectable nuggets that can add sparkle to a cold January day.

Indira Gandhi's comments on her contemporaries are a hoot. Of Harold Wilson she writes, 'I wish he had more sense of humour.' Of Lord Mountbatten, who she calls 'incorrigible': 'He is friends with all the wrong sort of people.' And of Morarji Desai, who at the time was threatening a fast unto death: 'Our difficulties are acute and varied enough without having a dead Morarji haunting the scene.'

The description of Subramanian Swamy, written in the middle of the Emergency, betrays as much of Indira Gandhi's own rancour as it captures something of the man. 'In India he has no influence whatsoever,' she starts. 'He has not been a success in the Parliament and there are often sniggers when he gets up.' Then she adds: 'He seems to have a complex of some kind and is aggressive in a defensive way, if you know what I mean.'

The letters reveal Mrs Gandhi had an impish sense of humour. Commiserating over Natwar's slipped disc, she says: 'Do you remember when the same thing happened to KPS Menon? He had to stand in a very artistic Ajanta pose for quite some time.' Of Pokharan: 'Our own blast has been successful, however, the blast from other countries is pretty strong and one does not know what the fall out there will be!'

Occasionally, Natwar's footnotes are most telling. In August 1980, just after Sanjay Gandhi's death when Rajiv was under pressure to join politics, Natwar wrote to him. Calling him 'the senior male member of the world's most distinguished, durable and famous political family', he adds, 'India needs you.'

Alas, the book does not contain Rajiv's reply but a footnote recounts something he said to Natwar: 'I am not Sanjay, besides I have no money, apart from my salary.'

However, it's the correspondence between Natwar as high commissioner to Zambia and Morarji Desai, then Prime Minister, that tells you most about the author. When Desai failed to thank Kenneth Kaunda, the Zambian President, for the praise he showered on Natwar, this is what the high commissioner wrote to his Prime Minister: 'The extreme austerity of your reply must make my task in Lusaka infinitely more difficult. I am sure it was not your intention to belittle or undermine the position of your high commissioner in Zambia, but such an inference can be drawn and is being drawn.'

Morarji was not moved. 'I am surprised you should attach so much importance to certificates from foreign dignitaries, you are needlessly sensitive about this matter and I am wondering how this sensitiveness fits in with the discharge of your duties as high commissioner.'

Undaunted, Natwar replied: 'You say that I am being "needlessly sensitive". Sir, I am glad I do not have a thick skin. My sensitiveness has never come in the way of my duty.'

Bravo Natwar!

4

Writing about Yourself

I'm sure you would agree that autobiographies are not easy to write. Even authors who have led fascinating lives are often mistaken about what events to include or judiciously omit, leave aside the degree of subsequent detail. Some start at the beginning and plod on to the end leaving you lost, bewildered or bored. Others skim or circumvent and end up offering an unsatisfactory and incomplete account. Most get confused between the personal and the professional.

Now, if you think about it, for these very reasons autobiographies are also not easy to read. You may be curious about the author but do you really want to know everything about him? On the other hand, how satisfactory is his self-serving selection of events and details? Without the benefit of an astute biographer's commentary, you either have to rely on your own sceptical judgement or simply suspend evaluation. Neither is easy or advisable.

This is why Fali Nariman's autobiography, *Before Memory Fades*, is a joy to read. No doubt the author starts at the beginning but it's not his life story he relates, so much as an honest account of the important events that stood out in his life. You can pick and choose the ones that interest you and you don't have to read them in any particular order.

However, *Before Memory Fades* is exceptional for two other reasons.

They're worth noting carefully in case you are, secretly or wantonly, planning an autobiography yourself. First, it deftly avoids the pitfalls most memoirs inevitably hurtle towards and second, it discovers the real secret of a delightful read.

The author doesn't blow his own trumpet although if he had wanted to, he could have played a fairly riveting tune. Thus, you only discover accidentally that in the 1980s, chief justice YV Chandrachud invited him to join the Supreme Court. A rare direct appointment from the Bar. At the time he was fifty-three. If Nariman had accepted, he would have ended up as chief justice and served an astonishingly long term. But he declined. Today, how does he look back on this? 'I comfort myself with the reflection that I would not have made a good judge.' Pleasing modesty which perhaps proves he's wrong!

The secret the author has discovered is that nothing is so gripping as a good story. And Fali Nariman certainly knows how to tell one. Lawyers, because they stand up and address a court for a living, have learnt to hold attention. When they don't, they usually end up losing! Fali Nariman's account of the Bombay Bar he joined in 1952, told through a series of stories about his mentor, Sir Jamshedji Kanga, is simply impossible to put down.

Actually what you don't realise, except in the company of lawyers, is that they have a fund of fascinating anecdotes and riveting tales. More importantly, they tell them with a sense of drama. They enact the different parts, their voices rising to a shattering crescendo or dropping to the softest sotto voce. It's an act, of course, but it can be spellbinding.

Each of his stories tells you something of Fali Nariman. He's not just the raconteur but the man in the middle too. However, what they reveal is what you have to work out for yourself. This is, therefore, an autobiography that makes you think. That, I would say, is the third Nariman 'trick'. The author makes you engage with the book rather than simply read it.

5

Jaswant and Jinnah

There's a book that deserves to be widely read and I want to draw your attention to it. It's Jaswant Singh's biography of Jinnah. Read on and you'll discover why.

Jaswant Singh's view of Jinnah in *Jinnah: India, Partition, Independence* is markedly different to the accepted Indian image. He sees him as a nationalist. In fact, the author accepts that Jinnah was a great Indian. I'll even add he admires Jinnah and I'm confident he won't disagree.

The critical question this biography raises is how did the man they called the ambassador of Hindu-Muslim unity in 1916 end up as the Quaid-e-Azam of Pakistan in 1947? The answer: He was pushed by Congress's repeated inability to accept that Muslims feared domination by Hindus and wanted 'space' in 'a reassuring system'. Jaswant Singh's account of how Congress refused to form a government with the Muslim League in Uttar Pradesh in 1937, after fighting the election in alliance, except on terms that would have amounted to its dissolution, suggests Jinnah's fears were real and substantial.

The biography does not depict Jinnah as the only or even the principal villain of Partition. Nehru and Mountbatten share equal responsibility. Whilst the book reveals that Gandhi, Rajagopalachari and Azad understood the Muslim fear of Congress majoritarianism, Nehru could not. If there is a conclusion, it is that—had Congress accepted a decentralised, federal India, then a united India 'was clearly ours to attain'. The problem: 'This was an anathema to Nehru's centralising approach and policies.'

Jaswant Singh's assessment of Partition is striking. After asserting it 'multiplied our problems without solving any communal issue', he asks, 'If the communal, the principal issue, remains…in an even more exacerbated form than before…then why did we divide at all?' The hinted answer is that no real purpose was served.

Jaswant Singh, however, goes further. He accepts that because of Partition, the Muslims who stayed on in India are 'abandoned', 'bereft of a sense of real kinship' and 'not…one in their entirety with the rest'. And he concludes: 'This robs them of the essence of psychological security.'

But that's not all. He does not rule out further partitions: 'In India… having once accepted this principal of reservation (1909)…then of partition, how can we now deny it to others, even such Muslims as have had to or chosen to live in India?'

Where the book compares the early Jinnah and Gandhi, the language and the analysis tilt in the former's favour. At their first meeting in 1915, Gandhi's response to Jinnah's 'warm welcome' was 'ungracious'. Gandhi insisted on seeing Jinnah in Muslim terms and the implication is he was narrow-minded. Of their leadership, the book says Gandhi's 'had almost an entirely religious provincial flavour' whilst Jinnah's was 'doubtless imbued by a non-sectarian nationalistic zeal'. Finally, in terms of their impact: 'Jinnah… successfully kept the Indian political forces together, simultaneously exerting pressure on the government.' In Gandhi's case, 'that pressure dissipated and the British Raj remained for three more decades'.

Unfortunately, I can't assess the reliability of Jaswant Singh's viewpoint. I'm a journalist not a historian. But I can assert that it's courageous and probably a valuable corrective. We need to see Jinnah without the hate or prejudice of the past. It may be uncomfortable to accept suppressed truths but we can't keep denying them.

This book will stir a storm of protest, perhaps most from Jaswant Singh's own party. He realised that. But it did not deter him.[1]

---

[1] Editor's note: This article was written on 25 August 2009. Jaswant Singh was expelled from the BJP in August 2009, shortly after the publication of this book. He was readmitted to the BJP in 2010 only to be later expelled in 2014.

6

King Charles III

If a play can prove that Britain is a truly exceptional country from which we have a lot to learn, then I believe I saw it not long ago in London. It's called *King Charles III* and it's a delightful, if contentious, flight of imagination about what could happen when the present Prince of Wales succeeds his mother. It played to packed houses at Wyndham's Theatre in London.

First, the 'facts'. The play begins with the funeral obsequies following the death of Queen Elizabeth. Charles, the new king, is torn between his duty to preserve the monarchy and his personal sense of commitment to uphold Britain's democracy, when the incumbent Labour government passes a bill effectively throttling the free press and thus undermining freedom of expression. King Charles refuses to sign and asks the Prime Minister to reconsider. But the Prime Minister digs in his heels and secures the support of the Conservative Opposition thus presenting the monarch with a united House of Commons behind the bill.

At this point, a conventional monarch would have accepted the will of Parliament and signed the bill into law, even if reluctantly. Charles, however, acts very differently. Citing an ancient medieval prerogative of the British monarch, he enters Parliament and orders the Speaker to dissolve the House. A fresh election, he believes, will sort out the dispute between the government and the monarch.

Though technically dissolved, Members of Parliament (MPs) refuse to vacate the House of Commons and insist on functioning as if Parliament is still effective. As a result, the Parliament and the monarch are locked in irresolvable conflict. The British constitution is under the worst possible strain.

The monarch, surrounded by his family, plans to address the nation to explain the steps he has taken. He believes this will be his coup de grâce. However, this is the point when Prince William, the new Prince of Wales, steps into the picture. Encouraged by his wife Kate and with the support of the prime minister, he manipulates the situation. Swiftly but secretly, he decides to speak first and announces his father's abdication. Then he signs the impugned bill into law.

Thus, ends the controversy Charles created. The longevity of the monarchy is ensured. The will of the Parliament remains supreme. The conflict between Crown and Commons is averted.

Now why does all of this prove Britain is exceptional? Because in no other kingdom would you see a play that starts with the reigning monarch's death. Where audiences flock to witness the heir apparent fail as king. Where the heir presumptive connives to replace his father to hurrahs from both the people and the Parliament.

Remember, the story is fiction but the characters are real. This play is an attempt to predict the future. And that future shows how King Charles, though well-meaning, could be a disaster. That William, though well-intentioned, is capable of virtual regicide and worse, controlled by his wife.

Finally but most strikingly, the play revolves around the anguish and later, the mental collapse of Charles as a person. Other than Britain, would any other monarchy accept this as legitimate, in fact popular entertainment?

In India, anything similar would be censored. Protestors would burn the theatre and lynch the actors. Politicians would scream treason. The press would cry blue murder.

In Britain, it's a roaring success. The play is sold out but no one has changed their opinion of Charles or William and certainly not of the monarchy. It's seen and accepted simply as a play. And that's it.

The Literary Indian

India never ceases to both fascinate and amaze me. About 35 per cent of the population may be illiterate, as per the 2001 Census, and a sizeable section of the remainder still struggle to read, and yet, tens of thousands crammed into the Jaipur Literature Festival, their respect for the written word and their curiosity and regard for authors as evident as their delight in sharing the company of the famous and the celebrated.

I'm not sure if there are many other countries where this would happen. I doubt if Britain, America or any major European nation would respond to a literature festival with such enthusiasm and self-evident enjoyment. And it certainly would not feel like a popular carnival. It would be far more sober and serious and perhaps, even pretentious. The crowds in Jaipur ensured that our literature festival was as much a tamasha as anything else.

Of course the critical question is whether the thousands in Jaipur were drawn by the books or attracted by the stardom.

Before I answer that question, ponder over this. Isn't it beguiling that JM Coetzee—and most of us can't even pronounce his name—or Orhan Pamuk, leave aside Chimamanda Adichie and Alex von Tunzelmann, should fill venues to bursting with no room left in the aisles and hordes still standing outside hoping to hear echoes of what was being said inside?

Even if they were only there to stare, to revel in rubbed off celebrity, it's incredible enough! Actually, it's almost unbelievable.

But, in fact, the audience, in January 2011, was attentive, thoughtful, responsive, critically appreciative and intent on absorbing each idea or thought they could grasp. What cannot be denied is that a very large number had come to listen and learn. They sat in total silence for a whole hour listening intently as Coetzee read. They were moved, literally to tears, when Izzeldin Abuelaish recounted his family's tragic plight at the hands of the Israeli army. And they enthusiastically questioned von Tunzelmann's account of independence and partition. In fact, where in the world would a historian speak to five or six hundred packed into a tent like sardines in a tin?

However, I can't also deny that several were there for the glamour. This becomes obvious when you find yourself stopped by a breathless gaggle—it could be men, women or school kids—clamouring for an autograph only to be asked, after you've signed countless scruffy scraps of paper, 'And who are you, Sir?'

Yet, I would add that it's the innocent and transparent joy of those who like to hang around the famous and often, sidle up for photographs or ask for messages to be inscribed on old and occasionally soiled programmes, that makes this acceptable, understandable and easily forgiveable. Indeed, it can be thrilling. Even infectious. I have no doubt if I'd spotted Coetzee, I would have spent hours queuing for an autograph on my tattered copy of *Disgrace*!

So what does this tell us about India? Of course, we chase fame and glamour but we also throng around writers and intellectuals and eagerly turn up for literary discussions or readings. Even when we don't fully understand or cannot easily follow, we're happy to let the flow of words and wisdom wash over us. I'd say it's like a dip in the Ganges. It leaves us feeling enriched, improved and full of merit.

Holy water may not be sufficient to wash away our sins but surely, literature and authors can only uplift our minds. Do you disagree?

8

Why I Like Khushwant Singh

I don't know him well but what I know of him I like. He's an engaging person. A man of stories, of delightful indiscretions, of loud asides and soft innuendos. What's more, he loves to talk. When he does, his eyes smile even though his face remains placid. And he knows how to tell his tales. They're full of delicious detail, parenthetical humour and clever turns of phrase.

Not surprisingly, he's an interviewer's delight. The publication of his long-awaited autobiography was a perfect excuse to ensnare him. But if I thought I had to lay a trap, I was mistaken. He accepted with flattering alacrity and even ducked an opportunity to question VS Naipaul to fit in with our recording schedule.

'So what's it to be?' Khushwant Singh asked as he walked into our studio. 'Most people think I'm a performing flea. Switch him on, get a few laughs, a few dirty jokes, a few caustic remarks and then switch him off!'

I had not thought of him as a performance-to-order nor I suspect did he mean to be. Humorists usually start by parodying themselves. Khushwant was simply getting into the mood.

'I want to talk about you,' I replied.

'Good Lord,' he said and laughed loudly, 'I'm not very interesting. Besides my best stories are about other people.'

He was wrong. Khushwant on Khushwant is irresistible. Not because he's bawdy or sensational, nor because he exaggerates or clowns around. But because it's the most honest I've ever heard him. In fact, excruciatingly so. The man that emerges is very different to the image we have of him. Very different to the picture he deliberately paints of himself.

We think of him as a modern-day Casanova. At his best a seducer of fair women, at his worst a pincher of voluptuous bottoms. He's neither. He's shy, timid and scared of being rebuffed. Maybe he is a voyeur—in fact he cheerfully admits to it—but he is no practitioner. And by his own admission, he is spectacularly lacking in prowess.

'I'd be quite happy to be seduced,' he told me. 'But I don't have the guts to seduce anybody. I don't have the nerve. If I was a man who made passes at women, I would have been slapped many times by now.'

The 'sexy' stories he tells are designed to enthral. He knows his audience and spins his yarns to suit their taste. Yet, sex and love have been the cause of pain, perhaps, even tragedy in his personal life. In his autobiography, he suggests his wife was unfaithful to him. I asked how painful this brief interlude had been.

'It wasn't very brief,' he replied almost matter-of-factly. 'It lasted nearly twenty years. You don't call that brief. It didn't get anywhere because I was there. Our marriage was a sort of roller coaster. There were times of deep discord. There were times of matrimonial bliss, to use a convenient Indian expression. And there were a number of times when we left each other to ourselves.'

This unhesitating confirmation stunned me. Even more surprising was the analytical, well-reasoned attitude behind it. There was no rancour or injured pride. Not much affection perhaps but no remorse either. I don't know anyone else capable of it.

'It's hard for me to judge whether I was good to her,' he continued. 'I did my best but it wasn't good enough, quite obviously.'

'Did she do her best to be good to you?' It was the obvious question.

'Well, she was convinced she was good to me,' he replied. 'Whenever we got into an argument, which was often enough, she used to dismiss it with a quotation from Guru Nanak. *Moorkh de nal na uljhiye* which means don't tangle with a fool. I was the fool.'

Khushwant's wife died in 2002. At eighty-seven, he too is looking into the abyss. In his autobiography he writes, 'I've dreaded death ever since becoming conscious of it.' I asked if that fear had got worse with age.

'I know the inevitable is close by now. The only thing I fear is the process of dying. I don't want to go in pain. I don't want to go in indignity. I don't want to be in a hospital with some woman putting bedpans under my bottom and then wiping it clean.'

He told me he's an agnostic. I asked if he was scared to die one. His answer mocked the gods we often unthinkingly rely upon.

'I'm agnostic to this day even though I don't know how long I have to live. I don't think God will be happy to see me when he does, if he is there to see me.'

I can't speak for God but we are not ready to lose him.[1]

[1] Editor's note: This article was published on 22 February 2002. Khushwant Singh died of natural causes at the age of ninety-nine, on 20 March 2014. He left in the way he wanted to go…

No Offence Please

Let's Face It: We, Indians, are a Highly Racist People

Let me start with a health warning: If you don't like reading criticism of the Indian people skip to another article. What follows is not just blunt but also reveals a dismal and depressing truth we rarely acknowledge. Yet, after the unspeakable treatment of a young Tanzanian student in Bengaluru we can no longer deny facts. Indeed, the time has come to confront the demons we harbour.

Are we racist in our attitude and behaviour? The answer is an unequivocal yes. We look down upon darker skins and discriminate against black ones. We call our own citizens from the North East chinkies and dismiss those from the South as Madrasis. And everyone from Africa is a *habshi*.

So deep runs our colour consciousness that even our celebrities are unashamed of it. How else do you explain the fact Shah Rukh Khan, Hrithik Roshan and John Abraham blithely advertise fairness creams and aren't embarrassed to do so? Can you imagine Tom Hanks, George Clooney and Brad Pitt doing anything similar? I suspect part of the explanation lies in the fact the rest of us yearn for milk-white brides and laugh away the moral issues that it raises.

Unfortunately, the problem has progressed beyond the attitude and behaviour of individuals. Our system condones it whilst those in authority seem to overlook it.

Both the Bengaluru Police Commissioner and the Karnataka Home Minister have refused to accept the traumatic treatment of the Tanzanian girl as a racist incident. The former preferred to see it as road rage. The latter as 'just a response to an accident'.

But why stop at them? Rahul Gandhi shied away from accepting it was racism whilst his mother was completely silent. That was largely true of Mr Modi too.

When Giriraj Singh said that if Rajiv Gandhi had married a Nigerian and not a white-skinned woman the Congress would never have made her President, the Nigerian high commission complained but Mr Modi forgave the minister.

In 2014 when Ugandan and Nigerian women accused Somnath Bharti of racism—and I believe he faces formal charges as well—Arvind Kejriwal stood solidly by him. At the time, Yogendra Yadav passionately defended him, though today he accepts that was a mistake. But Yadav is a rare politician to acknowledge the error of his earlier ways. No one else has.

Ask anyone who's served in Africa and you'll discover that Africans consider Indians more racist than the whites. Krishnan Srinivasan, a former high commissioner to Zambia and Nigeria, who also served as foreign secretary and deputy secretary general of the Commonwealth, unhesitatingly confirms this.

Even our greatest modern icon, Mahatma Gandhi, was guilty of racism in his early years in South Africa. Ashwin Desai and Goolam Vahed in their book *The South-African Gandhi: Stretcher-bearer of Empire* catalogue the many instances when his language or his actions betrayed deep prejudice against blacks. He called them 'Kaffirs'. In 1893 he wrote to the Natal Parliament comparing them to 'savages'. In 1904 he said: 'About the mixing of the Kaffirs with the Indians, I must confess I feel most strongly.' In 1905 he said he didn't want Indians and Africans 'herded together indiscriminately' in hospitals.

Let me conclude by saying our belief that we are tolerant and free of colour prejudice is an illusion. It's untrue. And it's only when we accept this fact that we will start to change.

Gandhi did and became a different man in his later years. The question is: Can we emulate him?

2

Disadvantage India

'What on earth is going on?' Pertie sounded intrigued but I could tell he was also exasperated. It was past midnight and there was an edge to his voice. 'Have we all gone mad?'

As you know, this is how Pertie's rhetorical conversations usually begin. So though I was tempted to reply flippantly, I bit my lip and kept silent.

'They're attacking women for drinking in pubs in Bangalore (now Bengaluru), in Bombay (now Mumbai) they're closing down shops called Karachi Sweets and banning the sale of Pakistani books whilst elsewhere courts are issuing notices to the producer of *Slumdog Millionaire* on the grounds the name is offensive. Doesn't it seem as if, suddenly, everyone's lost all sense of balance and perspective?'

'Oh come on, Pertie,' I replied soothingly, trying hard not to tut-tut. 'These are separate and isolated incidents. You can't add them all up!'

'And why can't you?' he shot back. 'Have you thought of the damage they've done? They're undermining the most important elements of India's image. First, Bangalore is supposed to be India's window to the world. It's thought of as modern, liberal and welcoming. Well, your Sri Ram Sena has effectively put paid to that. Now it's being compared to Jeddah, Khartoum and Tehran.'

Pertie, of course, has a point but I felt he was over-egging it. I tried to gently demur but I doubt if he heard me.

'Now turn to Bombay. First, they resort to blatant censorship and then, in the name of Indian nationalism, the twits from the Maharashtra Navnirman Sena (MNS) have ripped apart India's claim to be the original country of the subcontinent. The truth is it was all India before Pakistan was created. Pakistan, of course, doesn't always accept that and now the MNS has corroborated their view that the land west of the Indus is different and separate. What a fabulous own goal!'

This time I found it harder to disagree. But much like my earlier feeble interruption, Pertie didn't notice my silence. He was in full flow and like a steamroller, carried on.

'And then there's *Slumdog Millionaire*. After *Gandhi* in 1982, no film has done more to make the world aware of India. It's a runaway success. Yet, what's the response in India? Some foolish politicians think the name is offensive and at least one court has taken them seriously enough to issue formal notices to the producer! Talk about getting the wrong end of the stick.'

Suddenly the penny dropped. Each of these was bad enough on its own but together they made the outcome a lot worse. 'What's the world saying of us?'

'For many, we've become a joke. People don't know how to respond to girls getting beaten up for having a drink or shops forced to change their names because a handful of goons don't like them. They're laughing at us. But, sadly, the damage is deeper. It won't be long before people start asking awkward questions.'

'Oh,' I replied, mystified, 'such as what?'

'Such as India is supposed to be a tolerant, liberal democracy, so how come we can't accept a name like Karachi Sweets and buy Pakistani books? Or, Hinduism is supposed to venerate women; we supposedly elevate them to goddesses, so how come we thrash them if they walk into a pub? And then, India is supposed to be an aspiring and dynamic society, so, how come a rather clever name like *Slumdog Millionaire* can't be appreciated but is, instead, considered offensive? These are disturbing questions.'

'And how will they be answered?' If Pertie had further insights, I wanted to hear them.

'I don't know,' he replied honestly. 'But what I can tell you is that they underline the glaring difference between India and mature, self-confident countries. They're tolerant and accepting. We've just exhibited fatuous levels of intolerance and a perverse inability to accept recognition. It could make people realise that the real India is not in the smart-talking drawing rooms of Delhi and Bombay but in its insecure, quarrelsome backstreets and in the nitpicking litigations of its carping politicians. And if that happens, it could take the shine off the India story.'

3

Oh, to be in England Cracking Jokes about the Queen!

It's the perfect summer in London. Warm and sunny, the grass at Wimbledon is singing and the economy steadily rising. Even the Scottish referendum in September holds out little threat. Most people believe Great Britain will remain intact.

Consequently, the summer of 2014 is a glorious moment to catch Blighty at its best. I've just spent a week, which is far too short for a holiday but more than enough to appreciate the qualities of this sceptred isle. I want to write about one in particular and why I dearly wish we had it too!

The British have the most wonderful sense of humour. It's both funny—peculiar as well as funny—ha ha. That is to say, it spans wit and satire alongside ribaldry, pranks and silly jokes. The nicest part is that they laugh at themselves.

There is nothing the British cherish they will not also mock. A play called *Handbagged* deliciously illustrates this. It's the story of the relationship between Margaret Thatcher, Britain's first woman Prime Minister and the longest serving in the last century, and the Queen and it doesn't hesitate to send them both up.

How different we in India are! We laugh at others but never

at ourselves. The British have a sense of humour. We have a sense of self-importance. In fact, let's be honest, we're full of self-righteousness.

The Queen, as monarch, is both the epitome and the symbol of Britishness. Yet, her subjects frequently parody her accent, her manners and her clothes. And she wouldn't have it otherwise. For she knows that in such humour, lies true affection. In contrast, if you joke about an Indian politician, you could end up in jail. Our image is so fragile it can't take a little good-natured mockery.

If you're not convinced, let me offer another example. The Brits love their flag as much as we do. What's undeniable is that theirs is older, its history richer and it has represented their kingdom for longer. Yet, you can buy underpants and socks with the Union Jack all over them in Piccadilly. Tourists love wearing them. No one in Britain objects whilst crafty cockney shopkeepers make a fair amount from such sales.

Now imagine what would happen if the old *tiranga* were to be printed on socks and undies and sold on Janpath? And think how we would respond if American tourists pranced around wearing them? The RSS wouldn't be the only people to have a conniption.

The point I'm making is simple. You can laugh at someone and still respect them and love them. You can joke about them or mimic their behaviour without belittling them. Similarly, you can wear the flag as a shirt or boxer shorts without disrespecting it. It's entirely to do with your attitude and perception.

The opposite is also true. Just because you are silent and stand at stiff attention doesn't mean you respect the Prime Minister. Just because you bow and scrape doesn't mean you like him. And no matter how prolific the ceremony that surrounds the national flag, such displays of formality don't automatically amount to respect. They could be no more than just formality. Respect comes from the inside.

So the next time you visit London, spend less time shopping and a little more time observing. There's a lot we can learn from the Brits if only we would keep our eyes and ears open and our mind free of prejudice.

4

Richard, Shilpa and Young Mr Gandhi

If the lady who gets kissed doesn't mind—and for all we know, she may even have welcomed it—do the rest of us have any right to complain? I don't know about you but I would say no. Actually, I would say it loudly, unequivocally, publicly and repeatedly. And I hope the Shiv Sena as well as the more shrill brethren of the Sangh Parivar are listening.

So if Richard Gere should choose to embrace Shilpa Shetty and kiss her—once, twice or several times—and Shilpa accepts, then, as far as I'm concerned, you and I have no role to play. It's legal and it's moral. The question whether it's decent is for individuals to decide for themselves. There ought not to be a collective view of the matter. Certainly it's a lot less indecent than what Indian men do in public; be it scratching their genitals, urinating or defecating. And let us not even mention what they do in crowded buses to unwilling women who have little choice but to grit their teeth and put up with it.

However, let us for a moment become a little technical. First, what sort of kiss was it? As far as I could tell, it was on the cheek, friendly but neither intimate nor sexual and accompanied by a warm embrace. Was it embarrassing for others to witness? Would it have been unbecoming in front of children? Might it have been distressing for the elderly to see?

No, no, no—unless, of course, you're determined to take offence. If you are, the twenty-first century is not for you. It's not Richard and Shilpa who are out of place but yourself.

But hold on a moment. Before you take recourse to Indian history or culture, be warned. The India of the Khajuraho temples, Konark or the *Kama Sutra*—I wonder why they all begin with K?—is definitely not the sanctuary you are seeking. If I've read the book correctly, the *Kama Sutra*, is in part a manual on the art of kissing. Apparently, you can do it in 300 different ways. Alas, I'm only proficient in one of them! But if theory is not enough, Khajuraho and Konark show how it's done in practice. So, clearly our ancestors—peace be upon all of them—not only enjoyed kissing but adorned their temples with statues to immortalise the act.

I was in London and Milan when the brouhaha hit the newspaper front pages and television headlines. The only other story from India to merit similar attention was Rahul Gandhi's boast that his family deserved credit for taking India into the twenty-first century. The combination had my nephews chortling with laughter.

'Obviously the Gandhis didn't do as good a job as little Rahul thinks,' was Siddo's comment. 'Perhaps he should add a codicil the next time he addresses the good people of Uttar Pradesh. The Shiv Sena and Sangh Parivar are still stranded in the middle ages.'

'Or India's slid back!' Vikram retorted. 'Remember his claim that if the Gandhis had been in power, the Masjid would still be there? Well, now he can add that because the Gandhis aren't, India's dropped out of the twenty-first century!'

Which leads me to Gladstone and Disraeli. In the 1880s, they were political rivals. The former was obsessed with helping fallen women, the latter was known for his clever turn of phrase. In the middle of one of the many tightly contested elections they fought, Disraeli was informed there were rumours Gladstone had succumbed to temptation. In ministering to the women, he'd allegedly fallen for their wiles. Shouldn't the Conservatives use this to nail the Liberals, Disraeli was asked?

'On the contrary, not a whisper about it,' the worldly-wise politician shot back. 'If word gets out he's had an affair, he'll probably win the election. The voters would conclude he's human after all!'

This late Victorian story may be apocryphal but for me it's more twenty-first century than the rantings of the Shiv Sena and the Sangh Parivar. They're only of our age by accident of birth. Conversely, if young Mr Gandhi means what he says—and understands what he means—I'd like to see him speak out in favour of R&S. Not Rajiv and Sonia but Richard and Shilpa. Otherwise, his silence might suggest that he too is struggling to cross the millennium. He might have the intelligence but does he have the guts and conviction that characterise the twenty-first century?

5

Shame on Us!

The truth is we've become an intolerant people. When we don't like a film, we stop its screening. When we disapprove of a book, we ban it. When we disagree with someone's speech, we censor it. We forget that other people have different views, different tastes and different ways of doing things. Our way, we insist, is the only way.

Yet, we call ourselves a democracy and believe we uphold freedom of speech. But free expression is not just for those who we think are right. It's also for those who we believe are wrong. More critically, freedom of speech includes the right to offend. That has to be the critical test.

Sadly, that's where we fail. If Rushdie's interpretation of Islam upsets us, if Hussain's depiction of Hindu goddesses annoys us, if Nandy's analysis of caste and corruption raises troubling questions or if Kamal Haasan's *Vishwaroopam* disturbs our self-image, we turn on them with viciousness and vengeance.

The answer should be very different. If you disagree with something, counter it with fact and argument. If a book upsets you, write another. If a painting annoys you, don't see it. If a film troubles you, criticise it and if you can, counter its message with one of your own.

None of this do we do. Instead, we seek the easy but wrong solution: Ban the work, jail the author and wipe out from existence what you don't like.

Voltaire is supposed to have said, 'I disagree with what you're saying but I will defend to the death your right to say it'. We've changed that to, 'I disagree with what you're saying and you will die for it!'

Let's examine the Ashis Nandy incident a little closely, wherein at the Jaipur Literature Festival in 2013, Prof. Nandy is alleged to have made controversial statements about corruption among the so-called 'lower castes' in India. I concede that he expressed himself clumsily. I recognise that the point he was making was both complicated and for many, novel. It wasn't easy to grasp or comprehend. Many got the wrong end of it. Additionally, some television channels and newspapers misrepresented him by editing what he said and omitting the context in which he was speaking. And yes, those who know him say he has a penchant for speaking in surprising ways, even at times sensationally. So, perhaps, it was easy to misunderstand him.

However, once you realised you had, once it became clear he was making a very different point to what you initially thought, surely our response should have changed? But that didn't happen. We doggedly stuck by our initial impression even after it had been proven wrong.

But suppose for a moment we had been correct in our initial understanding of Nandy. Suppose he was out to offend. Does he not have a right to do so? Did that call for an FIR? Did that warrant the attempt to send him to jail?

Provided he was not inciting violence—and he wasn't, he was only speaking at a seminar in a literary festival—and provided he was not stirring up hatred which he clearly wasn't, he has a right to say what he wants. Otherwise, what is the value of our democracy? And our claim to champion freedom of speech?

The truth is this sorry affair reveals more about us than Nandy. We need to examine our behaviour. We need to question our responses. We need to ask whether we really understand what freedom means.

The Nandy episode and the treatment of Kamal Haasan's film diminish us. We're smaller because of our actions. We've shamed ourselves.

6

To Our Politicians—Please Stop!

I have a question to ask our politicians: Don't you have better things to do than work yourselves into froth about cheer girls? After all, you're not eighteen-year-olds measuring your lives with coffee spoons and if you don't know what that means, ask TS Eliot! You're adults. More importantly, you've been chosen to run this country. I would have thought inflation, farmers' suicides, urban crime, the Bus Rapid Transit (BRT) crisis in Delhi, the vanishing nuclear deal and the shifting political equations in Nepal—to name just a handful of the pressing problems India faces—would have kept you fully preoccupied. But I'm wrong. You've found time for the silliest of causes, something no one else had noticed till you chanced upon it and forced it on the nation. If this were satire, I'd say well done! Alas, this is reality.

And what is it about cheer girls that has got you so excited? Unfortunately, it's a mixture of prejudice, ignorance and balderdash. Some of you say they're vulgar. Perhaps, but does it occur to you that, like beauty, vulgarity lies in the eyes of the beholder? Many of us find your taste, behaviour and style vulgar but we put up with it. Is it too much to expect the same of you? That apart, do you know what vulgar means? The *Oxford English Dictionary* defines it as something that is patronised or practised by ordinary common people. Did you mean to be elitist or have you picked the wrong adjective?

Your second justification for banning cheer girls is they're un-Indian. Well, in a very literal sense, you're right. Until they were imported they were not known of by the vast majority of our countrymen. But that's also true of cricket. (Incidentally, I hope you don't think the game was handed down by the Vedas?) Yet, the fact that cheer girls attract attention by baring their midriffs and dancing suggestively is something we're very used to. Every woman in a sari has as much to show and reveal. Whilst Bharatanatyam and Odissi dancers—and let's not even mention Khajuraho and Konark sculptures or some of our delightful miniatures and the *Kama Sutra*—are far more sensual.

Those of you, who pretend to be moralists, have claimed cheer girls are demeaning of women. But if you think about it, you'll realise how silly that statement is. To begin with, the cheer girls are women and they're doing it willingly, even happily. Second, they're proud of the figures they're showing off. Third, the vast majority of the audience is enjoying their performance. This is not titillation. And though I don't deny there's a small perverted minority that's deriving pornographic pleasure, are the rest of us to be treated like school children because of this half per cent? Even you wouldn't say yes!

The most pertinent criticism is that cheer girls distract from the cricket. I have to admit there's probably some truth in that. Except what it overlooks, is that's precisely why they're there. T20 is not a test match, not even a one-day game. To be successful, a T20 tournament requires all the extras it can acquire. So, if you're a purist, it's not the cheer girls you should object to but the game itself. Don't expect the sobriety of Lord's when you're watching the thwack and shove of Yusuf Pathan and Brendon McCullum. Unless, of course, you're a hypocrite.

Actually, I'm afraid that's what it is: Hypocrisy. Bollywood indulges in crude and lascivious behaviour but you rarely, if ever, threaten to rip out those scenes. In fact, if I'm not mistaken, you court Bollywood stars and your ultimate goal is to get your kids to join them. Yet, if the rest of us have a bit of innocent fun, your moral hackles rise and you start cracking the whip.

Well, it's time you got off our backs. At last there's something on television the country seems to like and you have no right to ruin it. I suggest you grab a beer and enjoy the girls yourselves!

7

Grace in Defeat, a Lesson from Britain for Indian Politicos

I am an unmitigated—some would say incorrigible—anglophile and I've always believed there's a lot we can learn from this small island nation. For example, its humour and its willingness to laugh at itself, its talent for pageantry, the use of the understatement, West End theatre and the uniform high quality of its broadcast and print media. Now, let me add a sixth item to that list: The British knack for responding to political defeat with grace.

Within hours of the result on 8 May 2015—in fact even before the sun had set—three political party leaders resigned. They were Ed Miliband of Labour, Nick Clegg of the Liberal Democrats and Nigel Farage of the UK Independence Party. They accepted moral responsibility even though they were not personally to blame. They recognised the need for new leadership. They accepted that their parties cannot recover under a defeated and discredited leader.

How different that is to the way we respond. Sonia and Rahul Gandhi reduced the Congress to just forty-four seats but the very thought of resignation did not occur to them. Mayawati saw her party's fortunes reduced to zero but, unconcerned, soldiers on. The DMK was reduced to a mere rump in the assembly and obliterated in the Lok Sabha elections but the Karunanidhi family's control stayed unchanged. The CPM lost Bengal and Kerala and ended up with their worst Lok Sabha tally but Prakash Karat was unaffected.

I remember John Major's famous words at two o'clock in the morning when it was clear Tony Blair had swept the Tories aside. 'When the curtain falls it's time to leave the stage and that's what I intend to do. Tomorrow I shall be watching cricket.' Can you imagine any Indian politician similarly rising from the ashes of defeat?

What our politicians forget—but the British are all too aware of—is they have a limited shelf life. Once defeated the electorate deserves a new leader. That new leader has a right to refashion the party according to his or her vision. It's only then that a democracy provides a critical and meaningful choice. Simply recycling discredited leaders with the obstinate insistence that at some point the people will have to opt for them is to force yourself upon the electorate by wilfully denying them anything else.

I know Jayalalithaa can be cited as proof of the opposite because she's won three elections after three defeats. You could say the same of the Abdullahs or Mulayam Singh. But I believe they prove a different point about family-based parties or caste-based politics. Neither should have a place in a true democracy.

Finally, the British, you could say, are cruel to defeated leaders. When a prime minister loses he's moved out of 10 Downing Street within hours. It happens swiftly and smoothly.

Usually, defeat is clear by three or four o'clock in the morning. Around eleven o'clock in the morning the defeated prime minister leaves Downing Street for Buckingham Palace to hand back the seals of office. The movers arrive through the back door and clear out his belongings. After meeting the Queen he departs the palace in a courtesy car offered by Her Majesty. He's no longer entitled to the prime minister's limousine. And he heads for his own home. He cannot return to 10 Downing Street until he's earned the right to do so.

This speed maybe harsh but there's no room for misplaced sentiment in a democratic transition. The British understand that. Unfortunately, we don't.

8

We Need Cricketers Like Sachin but Definitely Not MPs!

I know I'm about to suggest irresponsible Members of Parliament are like errant schoolchildren but then, quite frankly, the requirement to attend Parliament is not dissimilar to the need to be present in class. In both cases, it's a moral responsibility.

PRS Legislative Research has analysed the attendance of MPs in the just ended budget session and found at least thirty-three who were present for less than fifty per cent of the sittings. In fact, a few were there for less than ten per cent! The thirty-three included MPs as supposedly responsible as the Congress deputy leader in the Lok Sabha, the Uttar Pradesh chief minister's wife and the Rajasthan chief minister's son.

However, I'm going to focus on Sachin Tendulkar. In the two years and four months he's been an MP, he's only attended Parliament on three occasions. Actually, a more appropriate word would be visited because he simply appeared, was noticed and left. He made no meaningful contribution. But attended is kinder.

The last sighting of Sachin-in-Parliament was on 13 December 2013. That's eight months ago. He sought and obtained permission to miss the whole budget session. In fact, by then he'd already been absent for over 90 per cent of the sittings. This means the next sighting of Sachin-in-Parliament won't be before the winter session starts in November. By then he will have been an absent MP for eleven months!

Sachin's excuse—and you'll soon see why it isn't an explanation—is that his brother, Ajit, has had heart surgery and he needed to be close by. That would be perfectly understandable but for the fact *The Times of India*, (on 9 August 2014) reported Sachin found time to visit England, watch cricket and holiday with his family. This was during the early weeks of the budget session.

What's worse is this excuse was made public during a visit to Delhi on Friday, 8 August 2014 for a Commonwealth Games felicitation function. If he wanted to, Sachin could have also visited Parliament. But he didn't. He came to Delhi but not to the Rajya Sabha!

Now I admit Sachin's behaviour is not unique. Rekha is another nominated MP who's gone AWOL (absent without official leave). Hema Malini and Tapas Pal are elected MPs who've also missed the entire budget session. Like the rest of them, Parliament is not a priority for Sachin. Being an MP is an adornment, not a duty or an obligation.

However, Sachin is different for two reasons and that's why I'm picking on him. And, yes, I admit I'm picking on him. First, he's an icon. Even Rekha cannot compare. And because he's so loved, he's expected to set an example.

Well, Sachin failed and undoubtedly, deliberately. For all his rhetoric of serving the nation—and he can be full of it—being present in Parliament, even in silence and even only occasionally, was a responsibility he was unwilling to fulfil. In fact, he consciously chose not to. And the only reason could be that it wasn't worth the effort.

Second, Sachin is the first sportsman to be nominated an MP. Actually, the 'rules' were altered to permit this. There was, therefore, an additional responsibility to justify the change. Alas, he didn't care. And the result? He's proved his critics right.

My conclusion is simple though brutal. Sachin has behaved badly. He's not only let us down, he's let himself down. And if, today, he's embarrassed by questions about his priorities, ethics and values, he has only himself to blame.

Sachin has diminished himself.[1]

[1] This article was originally published on 17 August 2014. The text here has been retained as originally published.

9

When It Comes to Our Chaps, the Joke's Never on Them

I don't think I'll ever stop marvelling at the stuff the internet throws up. Oh dear, that could have been better phrased! Every now and then I receive emails full of nuggets aficionados have dug up and salt them away for an occasion like this. Today, I'm going to share with you a small part of my collection and yes, I've phrased myself advisedly because I do consider them gems.

Unlike our politicians, American presidents have a tradition of self-deprecatory humour. The annual speech to the Washington Press Club is usually the occasion. But the idea of laughing at oneself in public goes a long way back.

This is what Abraham Lincoln said of himself in the 1860s: 'If I were two-faced would I be wearing this one?' A hundred years later, this is how Kennedy defended himself against the accusation he was using his father's money to buy the primary: 'I just received the following wire from my Daddy: "Dear Jack, Don't buy a single vote more than is necessary. I'll be damned if I'm going to pay for a landslide."'

Not surprisingly, Ronald Reagan was full of wisecracks. The wittiest was: 'I'm not worried about the deficit, it's big enough to take care of itself.' The cruellest was about the man he beat in 1980: 'Recession is when your neighbour loses his job, depression is when you lose yours and recovery is when Jimmy Carter loses his.'

However, perhaps the most truthful was this: 'I have left orders to be awakened at any time in case of a national emergency—even if I'm in a cabinet meeting.' But no one slept on the job better than Mr Reagan and the American economy loved it.

Lyndon Johnson's humour, like the man himself, was a touch rude but it made his point pretty effectively as this example proves: 'Did you ever think that making a speech on economics is a lot like pissing down your leg? It seems hot to you but it never does to anyone else.' By 1968, the country was so pissed off with him he decided to retire rather than stand again.

In these days of political correctness, presidential humour can't afford the sort of swipes Lyndon Johnson and Ronald Reagan were famous for. Now the butt of the joke is the President himself or the Presidency. Hence, Bill Clinton said: 'Being President is like running a cemetery—you've got a lot of people under you and nobody's listening.' Or Barack Obama: 'If I had to name my greatest strength, I guess it would be my humility. And my greatest weakness? It's possible that I'm a little too awesome.'

I suspect Jimmy Carter was being more truthful than witty when he said, a few years after he lost his re-election, to the same journalists who destroyed his Presidency: 'My esteem in this country has gone up substantially. It's very nice now when people wave at me. I notice they use all their fingers.'

Unfortunately, our politicians don't make jokes about themselves. Perhaps they fear we'll take them seriously and believe it's the truth! But the day Mr Modi or Mrs Gandhi laugh at themselves, even their critics could develop some affection for them. The point to remember is, when a person pokes fun at himself, he's rising above his critics and his problems without seeming defensive or smug. But unlike the rope trick, this is one we still have to learn.

The 'General' Idea

1

A Question of Generals

There's something about the title 'General' that puts people on their guard. Whilst kings and princes are held in awe and professors and doctors treated with respect, generals are feared. One doesn't brush with them lightly.

To be honest, I only found this out when I started to observe the way my friends would treat daddy. To me, he was my indulgent spoiling father. To them he was a General. So, whilst other dads were uncles, daddy was sir. It was an early reflection of a reality that I became increasingly aware of as I grew older: Generals are humans, no doubt but that only occurs to you when you get to know them. Till then there's an aura suggested by their title that creates a gap between you and them.

I am not sure how much of the press comment about Pervez Musharraf was consciously or unconsciously coloured by this fact although I suspect a fair amount would have been. But certainly the popular perception was deeply imbued by it.

'*Musharraf Sahab ka interview karoge*?' I was asked by a fellow customer at the barber's shop the day before the General arrived. I was getting my hair cut and he mistakenly thought it was in preparation for the summit.

'*Nahi,*' I replied trying to hide my disappointment.

'*Theek hi kiya,*' came the astonishing reply. '*Bade generallon se bach ke rehna chahiye.*'

'*Kyon*?' I had not meant to prolong the conversation but I was so taken aback by his comment, the question popped out involuntarily.

'*Pata nahin kya ho jayega aap ko. Aam neta ko naraaz kiya to woh bhool jayenge. Lekin agar kissi general ko gussa aya to museebat mein phas jaoge!*'

I've often wondered what element of a general's bearing creates this forbidding response in most people. Only a few of them have loud booming voices and not all are tall, strapping, imposing figures. Even when the odd one turns out to be supercilious, this aura is not punctured. The answer, I suspect, lies in their sense of style and possibly in their swagger. They exude authority, they are accustomed to be obeyed and there is little, if any, hesitation or false humility in their speech. They're not rude but they know what they want and it's pretty hard to resist them.

So, even when they are depicted in comic circumstances or do something silly themselves, it doesn't detract from the image we have of them. I first noticed this in Nigeria in 1979. I was twenty-five and attempting to hold down my first job whilst the country was in the throes of a general election and a long-awaited transformation from military dictatorship to civilian rule. The Second Republic was about to be born.

The general who was stepping down was Olusegun Obasanjo. Incidentally, he's back in power today, this time as a popularly elected civilian president but that's another story. At the time, he was still in olive green fatigues and his power came from his support inside Dodan barracks.

Now Obasanjo was the canniest dictator I have ever seen. He took to holding public rallies to acclaim the restoration of civilian rule. It was a bit like 'hail to the Chief' because soon the Chief will cease to be Chief. Millions would throng to hear him as he extolled the virtues of the very democracy he had so successfully denied his people in the preceding three years. It was the first and only time a dictator had proclaimed his own demise and enjoyed doing so.

The Nigerian papers were not sure what to make of it. But with their characteristic robustness, they decided to convert their dictator into a front-page pop hero. Film stars would have been envious of the treatment he received.

After one of the larger rallies, *The Daily Times* came out with the biggest headline I've ever seen.

'Obasanjo Exposes Himself,' it shrieked. I almost dropped my morning tea down my pyjama front. What followed was even better.

'Yesterday General Olusegun Obasanjo exposed himself to an adoring crowd on Marina Beach. After a one hour long standing performance that broke all previous records, they gave him the clap.'

We laughed for weeks but no one thought of General Obasanjo as anything but a tough officer and a stern forbidding presence.

Much the same is true of our generals. KM Cariappa was our first army chief. Decades after he retired, Rajiv Gandhi made him a Field Marshal. The day that happened, I remember being told an endearing story about him. Of anyone else it would have been an embarrassing exposé. Of Cariappa, or of any other general for that matter, it was simply a bon mot that reinforces the fact he was different to the rest of us.

Just before Independence in 1947, the story goes, Cariappa was addressing his troops. His aim was to translate into simple everyday language what freedom would mean. But like many of his generation this Sandhurst-trained officer had a less than perfect grip of the Hindi language. Enough, no doubt to address the army but nowhere near enough to know the subtle difference between the many synonyms for free that he could choose from. He chose the wrong one.

'*Kal mulk muft hoga,*' he said to his startled soldiers. '*Tum muft, hum muft, sub muft.*'

And then, raising a hand in salute and encouraging the assembled troops to reply, he shouted: '*Mufti ka jai!*'

For fifty years and more, this story has done the rounds and each time it provokes peals of laughter but not once, not even for a moment, has it changed anything about the way we think of Field Marshal Cariappa.

That, I suppose, is what makes generals special. Even their faults and foibles become part of the myth and romance that surround them. No wonder little boys like to dress up in military uniform and strut around. The only difference is generals do it for a living.

2

Fluffy Pillows, Peanut Butter and General Pinochet

I like to spend my Sundays in bed and on such occasions, I'm happy to be alone. In fact, company would be an encumbrance. Like a beached whale propped up against large fluffy pillows, I lie there watching TV and reading the papers or maybe it's the other way round. It all depends on how pleasant things were the night before.

Thus reposed, my mind flashed back more than twenty-five years. Now a quarter century is awfully long ago, particularly when you observe that most of you reading this piece weren't even thought of at the time. In fact, it's so far back that the story I have to tell might well be a fairy tale.

I was still in school, Edward Heath was Prime Minister (so too was Indira Gandhi) and Rajiv was just her son. A young, romantic President of Chile, Salvadore Allende, was the toast of the left. His victory in 1970 was proof that democracy and defiance were alive in South America. Of course, the Yankees to the north were livid but that only added to the atmosphere of heady exhilaration.

Allende's victory was the stuff of magic. It made the young feel mature, the old feel young, the cautious carefree and the headstrong responsible. It was one of those defining moments when everything changed. Hope was born and each day was a new dawn.

Then it happened. As the September shadows started to fall across the last hint of summer, a stern, rather too well-manicured general called Pinochet stormed the presidential palace in Santiago, murdered Allende and grabbed power. The right was back in office but this was no ordinary right. It was the spanking uniforms and polished brass of the Chilean army with Milton Friedman as their guru. An odd combination but it would in years to come be recognised as the crude start to a rightward shift in world economics.

In 1973, that was enough to bring students, idealists and trade unionists out on the streets. I was too timid or let's be honest too conscious of my amour propre to indulge in such histrionics but my sympathies were with Allende. Like everyone else, I hated Pinochet. I prayed for his defeat.

At the time, I was too young to know that only in scripture does good triumph over evil. In fact, with Diwali over, one can forget that illusion for another year. In life, the devil wins. 1973 was no different. Pinochet quickly established himself. His rule was unshakeable and he ruthlessly killed whatever opposition he encountered. So, it wasn't long before the protesters cried themselves hoarse, grew tired and then, finally, grew old. Or worse, they grew up and their teenage socialist souls changed into adult capitalist hearts.

Meanwhile, Chile prospered. In 1990, Pinochet, now an old but no less stern and still a hugely over-manicured man, retired handing over power to a carefully nurtured democracy. He granted himself amnesty and a lifelong position in the senate.

The Pinochet years were over; the Pinochet crimes, it was widely assumed, were forgiven or at least forgotten. Time, the influence of Reagan and Thatcher and the collapse of the Soviet Union had eroded or at least whitewashed the memories of a generation that had marched the streets of London mourning Allende and protesting Pinochet.

And then what do I discover?

As I lay propped up against the old feathers, peanut butter and marmalade sandwiches and masala tea at hand, my glasses perched on the bridge of my nose, I found that dear Tony Blair, never a leftie if he has a choice, had arrested Pinochet (on 10 October 1988). The old Chilean general, aged eighty-two, had flown to London for an operation and Tony had put the clamps on him.

I spluttered over my toast and tea, spraying the blanket with half-chewed junk food but I was delighted. Fate had eventually caught up with Pinochet. Good had asserted itself and God had at last triumphed.

I have no idea how it will end but my heart quickened, my pulse raced and my soul sang out—a bit too loudly for the neighbours but perhaps when they read this, they'll understand.

No longer am I a leftie, if ever I was one, but it's thrilling to have old idealisms requited. I feel a debt has been paid, a burden lifted, a commitment fulfilled. I had no idea that teenage passions could rekindle and that old fires could burn with such fury. Maybe this won't ever happen again, but as I rested on my pillows, stuffing my face, I felt the years fall by my bedside.

Who needs Viagra when the news is so uplifting![1]

[1] Editor's note: This article was published on 21 October 1988. According to the results of a 2011 investigation by a Chilean court, Salvador Allende's death is attributed to suicide. He died of self-inflicted gunshot wounds from an AK-47 rifle. Pinochet was released on medical grounds from house arrest in Britain and returned to Chile. He passed away on 10 December 2006, without having been convicted of any of the crimes of which he was accused.

3

Jacob's Jewels

Who'd have ever thought retired army generals spend their time trawling the net, discovering the witty or insightful comments of others and then circulating them widely to their friends? And certainly not generals who've played a critical role winning the Bangladesh war and then gone on to serve as governors of states like Goa and Punjab. But 'Jack' Jacob is definitely one such.

I'm a regular and grateful recipient of General JFR Jacob's tireless efforts. Depending on what strikes his fancy, his wide-ranging output keeps me variously informed, amused, appalled and occasionally, horrified. I've even based a few television current affairs discussion programmes on 'research' that he's sent me.

Today, however, I want to share what he calls 'ageless wit and observations'. It's a collection of pithy comments which the good general must have spent a fair deal of time digging out.

First, how has politics and government been viewed down the ages? As far back as 430 BC, Pericles had seen the truth: 'Just because you do not take an interest in politics doesn't mean politics won't take an interest in you!' By 1764, Voltaire had considerably sharpened his focus on the problem: 'In general, the art of government consists of taking as much money as possible from one party of the citizens to give to the other.'

A century or so later, George Bernard Shaw worked out the political logic behind such behaviour: 'A government which robs Peter to pay Paul can always depend on the support of Paul.'

But it was Winston Churchill who ultimately exposed the folly of believing that simply by taxing the rich, you can make everyone well-off: 'I contend that for a nation to try to tax itself into prosperity is like a man standing in a bucket and trying to lift himself up by the handle.'

The problem is our expectations of government. Ironically, it doesn't only make us secure. It can also make us vulnerable. As Thomas Jefferson put it in the nineteenth century: 'A government big enough to give you everything you want, is strong enough to take everything you have.' Ronald Reagan converted his admired predecessor's aphorism into the simple language ordinary citizens can understand: 'Government's view of the economy can be summed up in a few short phrases—if it moves, tax it; if it keeps moving, regulate it; and if it stops moving, subsidise it.'

The solution is a more cautious and less ambitious view of government. Keep it slim and limited. Omniscient government can be a monster. As PJ O'Rourke explained: 'Giving money and power to government is like giving whisky and car keys to teenage boys.' But if cautious handling doesn't work, then there is the artist Edward Langley's suggestion: 'What this country needs is more unemployed politicians.'

However, General Jacob's collection of witticisms is not solely targeted on politicians or governance. Another favourite subject is the press. He's no admirer of my profession and usually dismisses us as hacks. If you ask him what he thinks of newspapers, television and journalists, he will quote from Mark Twain: 'If you don't read the newspaper you are uninformed; if you do read the newspaper you are misinformed.'

In private conversation he's a lot sharper. Once, when I was disputing a point he'd made and quoted what I considered relevant facts, he shot back: 'If you've got that from a journalist, it's either exaggerated or downright wrong.'

I wonder how many of you agree?[1]

---

[1] This article was published on 10 September 2009. General Jacob passed away on 13 January 2016.

4

The Charm of the Generals

It's odd but Pakistan's military dictators tend to be more personable than its civilian heads of government. I never got to meet Ayub Khan but everything I've read and heard about him would suggest he was a bon viveur. Muhammad Zia-ul-Haq and Pervez Musharraf I've met and their charm is unmistakable and usually irresistible.

In contrast, the elder Bhutto and Nawaz Sharif may have known how to strike a rapport with a crowd but in intimate personal contact, they were lacking in warmth. In Nawaz's case, being Punjabi, what passed for warmth was hardly charm. As a woman, Benazir Bhutto is more difficult to judge. She retained a certain distance unless, of course, you got to know her well. But for most people, the gap was never bridged.

I first met General Zia in 1985. I was twenty-nine and visiting Islamabad to interview the dictator. He was at the peak of his power but attempting to disguise it by swapping his uniform for mufti. We met at the Army House. I was escorted into the drawing room by his ADC. The General was standing in the middle surrounded by officials, both military and civilian. At the corner of the room stood soldiers on guard. Their uniforms may have been ceremonial but their guns were clearly visible.

I entered and started the walk up to General Zia when, like magic, he swivelled around, smiled broadly, stuck out his hand and stopped me in my tracks.

'Welcome to Pakistan, Mr Thapar,' he said, with an aplomb that would do a PR man proud. 'Did you know I served under your father?'

I did not. More importantly, I wasn't prepared for such conviviality. I had expected a taciturn and stern general and had therefore, prepared my own opening gambit. Now it was redundant and with it my carefully nurtured confidence seemed to disappear.

'And how do you find our country?' The General continued perhaps sensing that at least conversationally, he had already got the better of his twenty-nine-year-old interviewer. 'Is this your first visit?'

I realised that I had to get back into the conversation. If I stood around stammering genially but embarrassedly, I would never recover my poise in time for the interview. It was important that I hit back with my own 'charm', such as it then was.

'I'm having a terrible time with my shower,' I blurted out without fully realising how odd that remark would seem.

'Oh,' said the General, his eyebrows rising and his voice a little incredulous. But I could tell that I had won back a little of the element of surprise.

'I can't get it to work properly, Sir,' I explained. 'It's very frustrating because as a result I don't feel I've had a proper bath'.

'You must complain,' said the General. 'I always do. When things don't work properly, I always complain.'

Imagine a dictator—even if he was one they used to call Terry Thomas—telling a journalist to complain? It made me feel very welcome but it also left me completely disarmed. Not a propitious start for what was meant to be a no-holds-barred interview.

Anyway, the job done and not too badly at that I got up to leave. The General rose too. He put an avuncular arm around my shoulder and escorted me to the porch. Then he leaned forward and opened the car door.

'Come again,' he said, as I stepped in, 'it was a pleasure.'

I was flummoxed but there was more to follow. The car circled the round front garden and as it straightened itself before heading for the gate, the General's ADC who was sitting in the front and therefore had his back to General Zia, suddenly spoke out.

'Turn around, Mr Thapar. The General is waving.'

There he was on the porch under the yellow light, his black sherwani silhouetted against the white walls of the house. He had been waiting for this moment. As I turned to see him, he waved and the car drove out of the gate.

Fifteen years lapsed between this meeting and the one with General Musharraf. That too was at the Army House but it was a far grander and more impressive one. This general was also in mufti but not in a sherwani. He had on a well-cut dark double-breasted suit, a cream silk shirt and a striking Hermes tie. Later the tie, as you perhaps know, became mine.

I first spotted him through the open drawing room door. We were inside setting up. The General was striding down the corridor outside with Major General Rashid Qureshi (he had been promoted from brigadier the same morning) following in his wake. He had removed his jacket and in his shirtsleeves he looked businesslike and young. To be honest, I'm always impressed by the sight of well-dressed men in their shirtsleeves. It seems to suggest diligence and dedication.

Ten minutes later, when we were ready, General Musharraf walked into his own drawing room. This time he had his jacket but he still wasn't wearing it. It was slung across his shoulder and he was adjusting the knot of his tie as he entered. Once again, it seemed informal and friendly. Maybe it was meant to. If so, it worked.

The advantage I had in meeting General Musharraf compared to General Zia was that being older, I was more observant, more able to assess a man's behaviour and style and less nervous or self-conscious of myself. As I sat opposite him, I first noticed his eyes. They seemed warm and friendly; at times, they almost seemed to smile. Then I became aware of his face. It stayed calm and placid and even when the questioning got tough, there were no signs of tension. Finally, I sensed his vibes. It's a dreadful word but I can think of no other to convey the ambience a man's behaviour can create. General Musharraf sends out good vibes. You can't help but like him. You want to trust him.

If I'm not mistaken it's this soft, understated, beguiling charm that Mr Vajpayee will also notice when he shakes hands with General Musharraf and sits down to talk with him. It's a type of charm he too possesses. They are both very charming men in the older and nicer sense of the term. Not PR slickness nor grand put-on gestures but warm human qualities.

I wish them luck. May they quickly like each other and want to trust the other.[1]

---

[1] This article was originally published on 28 May 2001.

5

The Weekend of the Generals

'Do you think it's just a coincidence?' Pertie suddenly asked. He has an irritating habit of popping questions without explaining what they are about. Fortunately, the mystery does not last very long. Pertie can't resist giving away his own game.

'This thing about their general and ours,' he added.

I could see that Pertie was struggling to convey his thoughts. The strain on his otherwise placid features was sharply visible. But I could also guess what he was getting at.

'I knew that Mush was a dab hand on TV but I had no idea our Paddy was equally good.'

Pertie paused to savour his thoughts. He likes to do that. But on this occasion, I must admit, he had a point. Now that he had expressed it, I realised I too was thinking along similar lines.

'The funny thing is that soldiers are not supposed to be gifted speakers. They're supposed to strut around with swagger sticks. They are supposed to be blimps. Yet, here we have two who are extremely impressive, convincing and seem to be sincere. It's odd, isn't it?'

I suppose it is. But it's not inexplicable. The coincidence maybe surprising but it only leads to a question I've often been asked before: What makes a person impressive on TV? Sometimes, people you least expect turn out to have the biggest impact. The opposite is also true. Those who you thought would carry great weight end up horribly disappointing. What accounts for this?

My answer is that television has more to do with manner, style and character than content and speech. It's a medium of the image not of the message. Or to put it differently, the message on television is conveyed by the impression you make and not just or not even necessarily by what you actually say. In fact, it's possible to say things your audience may not like or wish to hear and yet, come across impressively. Musharraf is the obvious example.

The truth is what you say is not as important as how you say it. What matters is whether you are smiling or scowling, whether your voice is relaxed or tense, whether your manner is comforting or disconcerting. The audience observes you—their eyes pick up the fleeting expressions on your face, the hair falling across your forehead, the wrinkles on your clothes or even the way you are sitting—and only then do they listen to you, if they listen at all. If your appearance is off-putting, your impact will be displeasing. That's not simply packaging and presentation. Musharraf's suits and natty ties reveal something of his personality that strikes a chord with audiences worldwide.

It's only after they've seen you that the audience starts to listen. But don't for a moment assume they will take in what you are saying. It depends on how you speak. Delivery is the art of winning attention, holding it and then conveying your message. Actual content is often secondary. Of course, the best delivery (and this is also true of great flights of oratory) cannot be devoid of substance. If it is, its impact will pall. But like candyfloss, taste can beguile before you realise there isn't more to it.

Bill Clinton is the obvious example. He both speaks well and has intelligent things to say. But even when his content is commonplace or obvious, he avoids trite clichés. That's why it's impossible not to listen. Perhaps a more telling example is General S Padmanabhan. As I watched his interview, I was fascinated by his smile. It conveyed two qualities simultaneously: Goodwill and menace. And he used it to great effect. It spoke even when his lips were silent or sealed.

General Padmanabhan used reticence as an inverse form of eloquence. His brevity was as articulate as General Musharraf's fulsomeness. Star News captured this brilliantly. Asked whether the Indian Army was prepared for a full-scale conventional war or if not, how long it would take to reach that position, the General paused before he spoke. His timing was perfect. Long enough to suggest he was taking the question seriously but not so long as to convey hesitation or uncertainty. The clincher was the answer itself. Just five words delivered with the merest hint of that famous smile. 'Yes, we are fully prepared.'

Pertie was right when he identified Mush and Paddy as masters of the skill of communication on television. They have style and a reassuring manner. They are easy to listen to, convincing and seem sincere. Since TV is about appearance, reality hardly matters.

But TV remains a difficult medium to master. You can be trained to be good but to be a star, you have to possess an additional, undefinable, God-given quality that cannot be mimicked or acquired if you don't already have it. Consequently, television likes some people and is kind to them. But there are others to whom it's unfair and often hugely so.

Richard Nixon was never comfortable and it showed. In turn, television was nasty. His five o'clock shadow, jowls and shabby suits conditioned his appearance. His incisive, analytical and often, forthright comments went unheard. If you watched the Kennedy–Nixon debates of 1960, he was the clear loser. But those who heard them on radio found him the obvious winner.

The opposite was true of Rajiv Gandhi. On radio where one is judged by speech and more importantly, content, he sounded naive, ill-informed and inexperienced which many, of course, thought he was. But on TV he was Prince Charming. Even his innuendos had the twinkle of captivating naughtiness. On his return from Sri Lanka in 1987, where Premadasa had publicly opposed the Indo-Lanka accord, he was asked if this undermined his achievement. At the time, Rajiv himself faced similar problems at home with Zail Singh. Smiling—and what a smile it was—he replied simply: 'Some Presidents have problems with their Prime Ministers and some Prime Ministers with their Presidents.' There was no need to say more.

This is why many who judge by television were dissatisfied with Mr Vajpayee. He was uncomfortable on screen and it was ungenerous to him. Each time he appeared, he added to our despondency. Perhaps it's unfair to judge in this way but what choice did we have? This is, after all, the age of television. And then however, we had someone who could gladden our hearts. No longer would General Musharraf steal the TV show, we had Paddy to speak for us![1]

[1] Editor's note: General S Padmanabhan was Chief of Army Staff of the Indian Army from 30 September 2000 to 31 December 2002.

6

The Major and the General

Are you aware the defence services regard politicians with contempt? In daddy's time, they used to refer to them as 'dhoti-kurtawallahs'. Since then the Sandhurst accents might have disappeared but the sentiment remains unchanged. The army, the navy and the air force are equally convinced that politicians enjoy cutting the services down and worse, they're reluctant to defend them.

Jaswant Singh's treatment of the Army Chief is a telling illustration of this. Not only was Singh wrong but he was also guilty of dragging General Deepak Kapoor into an unseemly and unnecessary controversy. As a former Defence Minister and an Armoured Corps Major, he should have known better.

In an interview to me in February 2008, the Army Chief[1] said there was 'a degree of misperception' behind the recent press concern with Chinese incursions. Explaining that China and India have 'different perceptions of the Line of Actual Control', he added that when China patrols up to the full limit of its perception, India considers that an incursion and vice versa. 'We would be as much blameworthy for that kind of incursion,' he stated.

This, of course, is the truth. More than that, it's time someone allayed

---

[1] General Deepak Kapoor was Chief of Army Staff of the Indian Army from 30 September 2007 to 31 March 2010.

the growing concern before it turns to anxiety. And what could be better than the Army Chief, the man ultimately responsible for the nation's security, doing this?

Alas, 'Major' Jaswant Singh disagreed. Describing the General's comments as 'unwanted, unwise and irresponsible', he added they were 'unbecoming'. Singh's case, as far as I can tell, was that borders aren't a matter of perception but determination. But the problem is that large chunks of the India–China border are not undisputedly determined. That's why there is a dispute. And at the core of that dispute are different claims of where the line lies. Now, if I'm not mistaken, that's another way of saying perceptions differ!

Of course, the Major's criticisms of the General did not stop at this. He accused him of 'engaging in…(a) free-for-all on television about Pakistan, China and the situation in Jammu and Kashmir'. However, the one thing you cannot accuse General Kapoor of is a 'free-for-all', whatever that silly phrase might mean. Not only was it a tightly scripted interview in which a free-for-all would not debut, also the General (unlike the Major) spoke in very precise and carefully chosen terms. Of course, the Major would have realised this had he seen the interview. But as he himself admitted: 'I did not witness it because I am not (an) avid viewer of television.' If only he had, he might have reconsidered his criticism.

Unfortunately that did not stop the Major going yet further. He also claimed General Kapoor's statements were 'harmful for the dignity not just of the high office that he holds but also for the total responsibility that he carries and for the security of the country'. That's rubbish. But what was true is that the Major's public attack was 'harmful' to the 'dignity' of the army chief's office. Major Singh, it would seem, was guilty of degrading the army chief's dignity, not General Kapoor!

But then the Major was a politician and the General was not. Perhaps that distinction also explained the response of the then Defence Minister and the rest of the government. Rather than defend his army chief, Mr Antony took recourse to silence. Worse, unnamed colleagues in the cabinet committee on security expressed criticism, thus adding to the Major's ill-considered comments. So, are you surprised the services look upon politicians as a rum lot?

And if you think I've picked a poor example or I'm exaggerating, ask yourselves why it's never occurred to any of our politicians to award Field Marshal Manekshaw the Bharat Ratna. Forty-five people have got it but is there even one amongst them who deserves it more? Certainly, there are several who should never have got it at all.

If the Major wished to atone for his lapse, I would suggest he take up this cause instead. If he does, all three services will thank him. At the moment, they have very different things to say.

Strictly Politics

1

Why Modi of 2017 is Not Modi of 2014

As he completes three years in office, there's no doubt the Prime Minister is a colossus amongst politicians. Not only is this obvious, it's probably unchallenged. However, that still leaves open the question, do you admire the man at the top or do you have concerns about his behaviour and statements? Each of us has his own answer and few would deny it divides us.

As I ponder over the significant impact the Prime Minister has made, I'm struck by a revealing, if not also novel, paradox: Mr Modi's strengths also metamorphose into his weaknesses. This means the same evidence can often lead to opposite conclusions. What I dislike, someone else will, perhaps, admire and what they find regrettable I, probably, see as a boon. Now let's explore this a little further.

The vast majority of the Indian people believe in Mr Modi. They feel he understands their needs and are confident he'll deliver. Not since Indira Gandhi has such faith been invested in the ruler of the country. As it was for her, this is one of his great strengths.

The flip side is that often Mr Modi gives the impression he knows best. It's said he's a good listener but frequently his mind is already made up. Demonetisation is the best example of a needless decision forced through because of his personal conviction. But not for a moment will the Prime Minister accept that.

A second strength is Mr Modi's capacity to take bold and radical decisions. We may have seen more in the foreign policy arena than in the handling of the economy but each time they've captured the imagination of the country. They suggest a strong, even courageous, leader. People like that. The smack of strong government is for many reassuring.

The obverse is that Mr Modi can be authoritarian. He *is* the government. The Cabinet is just the supporting cast surrounding him. A few, in fact, are no better than the gravediggers in Hamlet! But, again, wasn't this true of Indira Gandhi? Indeed, of all bold and decisive rulers?

Mr Modi's third strength is his gift for easy and fluent communication. It's not just that he speaks well but he also has the capacity to convey complicated concepts or politically awkward positions in simple and appealing terms. I cannot recall any previous prime minister possessed of the same skill.

Yet, this is also why Mr Modi's carefully chosen and deliberate silences provoke criticism. He's a natural talker, so when he doesn't speak, his reticence is viewed as crafty strategy. His critics, therefore, believe he is complicit in the darkening mood of the country. For many, this is perhaps the greatest fault they find in him.

Meanwhile, in one important respect, the Prime Minister is a different man to the one sworn-in three years ago. He no longer identifies himself with aspiration and the fulfilment of suppressed ambition. That, of course, was the promise that swept him to power, but he now seems to have cast it aside. Instead, today, he's become a tribune of the people. He identifies with the poor and the downtrodden. They are, of course, the majority and this explains the repositioning of his image. And who can say it doesn't make undoubted political sense?

But I, at least, am sorry to see the old Mr Modi fade away. In 2014, his vision had a strong moral content. Three years later, transformation has ensured it endures but it's also become pragmatic.

2

Advantage Mrs Swaraj

Has Congress overplayed its hand against Vasundhara Raje Scindia whilst throwing away the trump it could have used against Sushma Swaraj? I'm tempted to say yes.

Let's start with the case Congress has built against Vasundhara Raje. First, it accused her of impropriety because she provided a secret witness statement in support of Lalit Modi's application for permission to stay in Britain. But just because she's the Leader of Opposition in Rajasthan, is she precluded from standing witness for a friend in her individual capacity? No matter how unsavoury the friend and how undeserving his case, standing by him, if she so chooses, is her prerogative.

Of course, she should have made it clear she was acting in her personal capacity. Foolishly, she didn't. However, that's lapse of judgement, not a felony.

But then why did she want this kept secret? That's a critical question. Here's one possible answer: Because she had already experienced Congress's vindictiveness when it instituted the Mathur Commission to investigate trumped-up corruption accusations against her, which she fought all the way to the Supreme Court to have it struck down, and didn't want to provoke another burst of similar harassment. Even if you don't accept this justification, you can't say it lacks credibility.

Perhaps, because it agreed with the above arguments, Congress chose to target Vasundhara's son's business dealings with Lalit Modi and in particular, the question of who owned Dholpur City Palace. But this is where it went off the rails.

First, Congress got enmeshed in the technicalities and legalities of tax and company law, which are hard to follow but easy to dispute, and then it got caught up in a war of ownership documents, which proved nothing but only confused the picture. For all his showmanship, Jairam Ramesh wasn't convincing. Of course he was entertaining but he was also often contradicted.

Now, come to Sushma Swaraj. First, as External Affairs Minister she used her influence to help a man, whose passport had been revoked, obtain a British travel document, thus undermining the Indian government's decision to revoke his passport. That looks like abuse of power. Second, the man was her husband's and daughter's client. This seems to be conflict of interest. Third, a year earlier her husband had approached this same person for help in obtaining a place at a British university for his nephew. Arguably, that suggests quid pro quo. To my mind, this adds up to three good reasons why she should resign or be sacked.

However, there's one more. It could be the clincher. Section 13 (1) (d) (iii) of the Prevention of Corruption Act reads: 'A public servant is said to commit the offence of criminal misconduct if he, while holding office as a public servant, obtains for any person *any valuable thing* or pecuniary advantage *without any public interest*.' In Lalit Modi's circumstances, a British travel document was a very valuable thing and as far as India is concerned, no public interest whatsoever was served by helping him obtain it. In fact, you could claim public interest was undermined by helping him secure travel papers.

Heaven alone knows why Congress chose to target Vasundhara, against whom the case is only suggestive and therefore, hard to prove, as it turned out to be, and ignore Sushma, who was a sitting duck waiting to be shot down. If it ends up without the scalp it so desperately seeks, it can only blame itself.

Meanwhile, Mrs Swaraj must be very grateful.

3

The Importance of Being Shashi Tharoor even if Congress Disagrees

I want to write in Shashi Tharoor's defence. And I certainly hope that's how he views it. For Shashi is a friend, a valued guest on my show and an engaging writer whose books and columns I've enjoyed reading.

So, when Kerala Congressmen accuse him of being a fortune hunter, of flattering Mr Modi and surreptitiously implementing the Rashtriya Swayamsevak Sangh's (RSS) agenda, I'm bewildered. That's not the Shashi I know. But I'm equally stumped by his riposte. He's not an outsider and definitely not a foreign object. He's simply different. And thank God for that.

Now what is it that Shashi has done that's worked his partymen into such froth? In June, in an article for *The Huffington Post*, Shashi wondered if the new tone, style and behaviour of the Prime Minister adds up to 'a Modi 2.0, a very different figure in government from the ogre some of us had feared and demonised for years?' His answer was, 'It is still too early to tell but the initial signs are encouraging.' At the time, many would have agreed.

And then Shashi was invited by Mr Modi to be one of nine Swachh Bharat ambassadors. He tweeted he was honoured to accept, calling it 'a great campaign' but adding the challenge was to sustain it. But did anyone think the campaign was a bad idea? Sceptics said it wouldn't succeed whilst cynics called it a gimmick. Perhaps. But no one said it was wrong for the Prime Minister to campaign in favour of cleanliness.

On both occasions, Shashi said aloud what you, I and many other sane and sensible people said in our homes or, in my case, in TV studios: That the PM had made a good start, sounded different to the past and we, therefore, dearly hoped he was a changed man and that Swachh Bharat was a welcome attempt to clean our cities and change mindsets and habits, even if it was just a start without adequate backup in terms of structural reform.

The only thing is, Shashi is an opposition politician and spoke in public. The rest of us did so behind closed doors to trusted friends. That, quite frankly, was the error he made.

In India's partisan politics, any praise for the other side, even if slender and conditional, is an anathema. It's suggestive of floor-crossing. When it concerns Mr Modi, the impression the PM is succeeding or at least, not floundering makes it decidedly worse. How Congressmen wish he would, instead, stumble and collapse. They loathe him just as passionately as he hates them. The difference is Mr Modi won the election.

So was Shashi naive? Recklessly honest? Blindly, even unthinkingly, courting trouble? In the black and white world of Indian politics, where loyalty to one's side is valued more than the capacity to rise above the fray and recognise truth, you could say yes. But I would differ. Not because I disagree but because the time has come for change.

Shashi was attempting that. This is why I said he was different and thanked the good Lord for it. We need more politicians who can see the good on the other side of the aisle without switching sides or compromising the key principles which define their own position.

A little bit of bipartisanship doesn't weaken the political debate but it does enrich the nation. I hope Sonia and Rahul Gandhi are able to understand that. If they are, Shashi has nothing to worry about. If not...

4

Modi's Right, Do Not Politicise Triple Talaq

It was an odd subject for Pertie to raise. To be honest I wouldn't have thought the issue interested him. Yet when he called, his concern was unmistakable.

'Was the Prime Minister right to raise triple talaq?' he bluntly asked. Unprepared I played for time. 'Why do you ask?'

'Well, it's simple really. Is triple talaq a personal matter best left to individuals to decide for themselves or does it raise human rights issues where the State has a moral duty to step in?'

This struck me as a clear-headed and, even, insightful way of viewing the matter. Pertie had framed the triple talaq controversy rather cleverly and, when put this way, the answer was for me, at least, pretty obvious.

No doubt each time triple talaq is uttered, it only affects the lives of two individuals, but you also can't deny it transgresses fundamental rights which the State is expected to defend. Furthermore, if you believe in the sanctity of marriage then the arbitrary and peremptory character of triple talaq has to be unacceptable. If marriages have to be registered and recognised by the State then divorce must also have similar sanction. It cannot be left to the whims of individual husbands.

On all of this Pertie and I found ourselves in easy and quick agreement. 'So what about my question, which you still haven't answered? Was the Prime Minister right to say triple talaq mustn't be politicised?'

Undoubtedly he was. If triple talaq infringes human rights we value and the State is expected to uphold, it must not become an issue on which political parties take opposing sides. In a democracy you cannot defend a practice that is an affront to the Constitution, not to mention the very concept of justice.

'In which case would you go one step further? Not only should triple talaq not be politicised but it also must not be viewed through religious eyes?' This wasn't such an easy question to answer and I had to think carefully before I even tried. In the end Pertie answered it himself.

'If triple talaq offends against constitutional rights or the concept of justice, can we accept and accommodate it on the grounds Islam has sanctified it without diminishing our democracy? And, anyway, are you sure triple talaq is part of Islam? Scholarship is clearly divided on this. Indeed there are many Islamic countries where triple talaq is simply not permitted. So the claim India's secularism requires the State does not interfere with triple talaq is unconvincing.'

So far Pertie's logic was impeccable. I couldn't disagree. 'But don't we need to give the Muslim community time to accept this logic rather than impose it on them?'

'Why?' he responded. 'India didn't hesitate to outlaw discrimination on grounds of caste and, if anything, caste is integral to Hinduism. Why should triple talaq be placed on a different footing?'

Again, Pertie was right. If religious custom or observance flouts constitutional rights, the Indian State must uphold the latter. Minority faiths cannot be an exception.

Finally, Pertie's logic hinted at a further disconcerting question. On the issue of triple talaq, the silence or ambivalence of Congress politicians and those from the Left is disturbing. I accept this is an awkward issue but that's also why they need to speak out forcefully and clearly. There are times when you need to stand up for what you believe in. If you duck, it can only be at your own moral cost.

5

Suspension of MPs: A Very Healthy Precedent Set

Did the Lok Sabha Speaker murder democracy when she suspended twenty-five Congress Members of Parliament (MPs) for five days for repeatedly and defiantly disrupting the House? Or was she belatedly but necessarily, exercising powers that in fact should have been used decades earlier to enforce decorum and discipline? These are the two questions that frame the debate that followed the suspensions.

My answer is simple and straightforward. The Speaker did the right thing. And, yes, she and her predecessors should have exercised this power a lot earlier as well. But as they say, better late than never.

The critical issue is why do I say this? Let me explain and then illustrate how this sort of disciplinary action is standard practice in mature Western democracies, which we seek to emulate but mostly do not.

Parliament is the temple of democracy and debate and discussion is its raison d'être. This is how the legislature should make the executive accountable. Obstruction or disruption can only be accepted when debate has failed. Not as an alternative to, and certainly not in preference to, discussions.

Sadly, our MPs—and both sides are equally guilty of this—have chosen obstruction ahead of discussion. In doing so, they've turned parliamentary logic on its head. The BJP did it during the UPA years. Now the Congress is paying them back in the same coin.

In these specific circumstances, the government's willingness to debate including a prefatory statement by Sushma Swaraj and even, perhaps, the Prime Minister, was an opportunity for the Opposition to shame the government into sacking the allegedly errant ministers through the force of their arguments. It left no justification for obstruction. Alas, Congress made the wrong choice and the suspensions that followed were, therefore, the right response.

Now the challenge before the Speaker is to prove that she is even-handed and will hold the treasury benches to the same exacting standards of decorum and discipline as she did the Opposition. The next time BJP MPs disrupt, they must be suspended or the Speaker will justifiably be accused of partisanship.

Two years ago, I visited Australia and witnessed question hour in their House of Representatives. I'm repeating what I wrote then so you can see how strong Speakers impose discipline even at the cost of admonishing the Prime Minister:

'On 19 March 2013, the PM (Julia Gillard) responded to a question from the Opposition Leader with a snide remark about his alleged misogyny. This brought the Manager of Opposition Business in the House to his feet demanding she withdraw. However, he shouted out his last few sentences. Immediately, without even a second's hesitation, the Speaker ordered the Manager of Opposition Business to leave the Chamber. Without demur, he instantly did.

'Then, turning to the Prime Minister, the Speaker asked her to withdraw her comment. This was the PM's response: "If the Leader of the Opposition is upset in any way then I withdraw." Unsatisfied, the Speaker sternly rebuked the PM: "The Prime Minister will withdraw unreservedly." The PM, however, hesitated. "Order!" the Speaker barked. "Would the Prime Minister withdraw?" Admonished, she did. Softly, but clearly, the PM said: "I withdraw". The Speaker thanked the Prime Minister and continued with the business of the day.

'I couldn't believe the way the Australian Speaker had handled not just the Opposition front bench but the Prime Minister herself. Could such a thing ever happen in India? I asked myself.'

In August 2015 it did. I now hope this is a precedent that is used impartially and even-handedly.

6

Cry My Beloved Country—or Not?

I'm not just confused, I'm also shaken and upset. To be honest, I cannot understand what's happening around us. I know the depressing details and I'm aware of the apprehensions they've aroused but I remain uncertain of what to make of it all. So, today, I intend to explain my conflicted emotions and ask if you share them.

For all our limitations, contradictions and faults, I've always believed we're a tolerant people. We may have our differences and quarrels but for generations, multiple castes, creeds and cultures have lived comfortably together. Ethnicities, religions, languages and cuisines may distinguish and separate us but we've found ways of bridging the divide. This unity in heterogeneity is the silken bond that, unsung and often unrecognised, yet gently but usually firmly, binds us together.

That, after all, is what I was taught at school. This was how, with pride, I spoke of India during my years abroad. Seen in terms of our communities and cultures or our languages and regions, we may be different people, but hovering above this, there is an emotion, an affinity, a spirit that renders us one.

These days, it seems that invisible binding thread is coming loose. The sense of being one—though we are different in look and language, faith and fortune—is weakening. The feeling of being united is fracturing as the assertion of different identities seems more important.

Or else how do you explain the murder of a fifteen-year-old boy on a suburban train because his fellow passengers were provoked by his Muslim appearance? Or the lynching of a local police officer on the most holy night of *ramazan* by a mob comprising his own kith and kin? Or repeated vicious attacks on men lawfully transporting cattle on the unverified suspicion they could slaughter them? Or decisions that people who won't say 'Bharat Mata ki Jai' or choose to applaud a Pakistani cricket victory are guilty of sedition?

I could go on but I'm sure you've got my point. These developments don't just contradict our self-image but betray and undermine it. If it was only one or two occurrences, and only few and far between, you could explain them away or call them aberrations. But they're not. They're happening every day and all over.

Now do you see my concern? What does all of this add up to? What does it suggest of our country? Of what's happening to it and what, as a result, it's becoming? These are troubling questions and I don't have the answers. Nor do I want to accept the quick and easy ones that are sometimes offered. They point to an approaching darkness and they hint at the triumph of our inner demons and, perhaps even, the transmogrification of ourselves that I passionately do not want to see.

So, am I in denial? Or am I exaggerating my fears? I just don't know. Of course, I have my suspicions but can they—should they—determine my outlook? My view of my own country? And of my fellow countrymen? Again, I don't know.

Yet, of one thing I'm sure. At the moment this is not the country I thought it was. The India I love and will always be proud of appears to have receded. I hope this is because a light bulb is flickering and my vision has blurred. In fact, I'm still waiting for the power supply to steady itself. But am I waiting in vain?

7

Trying All the Wrong Things before Doing the Right One

The battle lines in Parliament are firmly drawn. I suspect a war of attrition will be fought in the Rajya Sabha between the government and the Congress party. I don't see the Upper House functioning, at least, not effectively, because neither side is likely to give up.

However, beyond politics, there is an interesting issue at stake. What is the greater priority for Parliament—debate, discussion and legislation to ensure good and effective governance or scrutiny of the executive with a primary focus on ensuring accountability and transparency? Even if that is not how either side frames the dispute, it's the important issue that underlies it.

You could answer this question either way. If Parliament does not legislate, laws will not be made nor reforms effected. Legislation is, therefore, the bedrock on which good governance has to be built. This argument leads to the conclusion that, above all else, Parliament must function with decorum and hopefully, efficiency and effectiveness. Supporters of the government will no doubt be on this side.

There is an alternative view and it's equally compelling. In our system of separation of powers, governance is the prerogative and responsibility of the executive. Parliament does not govern. It sanctions, legitimises, questions and most importantly, holds the executive to account. It, therefore, follows that making the executive accountable and transparent through its scrutiny is arguably the first priority of the legislature. This must be the Congress's defence.

Seen in terms of the second argument, Sitaram Yechury had a telling, if not convincing, point to make when he argued that discussion is not a substitute for investigation. All Members of Parliament can do is discuss, debate and pass resolutions. But the government, particularly when it has a majority, can ignore all of that.

What's needed, if we're going to get to the bottom of Vyapam as well as l'affaire Sushma Swaraj–Vasundhara Raje, is a focused, independent, professional probe. Only the executive can order that. Second, if it's to be meaningful you could, additionally, claim that the ministers concerned must step aside lest their continuation in office prejudice the inquiry.

So now you come to a position—assuming you agree with this line of argument—that the priority for Parliament is to encourage or coerce the government into holding an investigation. That is how, in this instance, Parliament will fulfil its duty to scrutinise and hold the executive accountable. And if obstructing the functioning of Parliament is the only way that investigation can be ordered, then that obstructionism is legitimate and justified.

Before you start to disagree, let me add that Arun Jaitley, in 2011, agreed with this logic: 'There are but rare occasions in history when parliamentary obstructionism is a part of legitimate parliamentary tactics.' At the time he had Andimuthu Raja in mind. But now, when it's the Congress's turn, surely the same logic applies to Chouhan, Swaraj and Raje as well?

Finally, the truly sad part of this mess in Parliament applies as much to 2011 as it does to events today: Why should obstructionism be necessary when simple common sense and decency should have produced the same result?

Sadly, in India we have to go to extremes to ensure the right thing is done. We don't do it automatically or quickly. We have to be pushed. That's why our Parliament so often seems dysfunctional before it corrects itself. To misphrase Churchill, we try all the wrong things before we end up doing the right one.

8

Modi and Dress Diplomacy

What has Mr Modi got against ties? Is it okay for the Prime Minister to dress 'inappropriately'? And is this a suitable subject for public comment? These are the three questions I wish to tackle.

Let me however begin by acknowledging I'm treading on controversial territory. There are many people, not all Modi supporters, who believe that criticism of how a man dresses is an unwarranted intrusion into his privacy or an unjustified comment about his personality. I believe that's true of ordinary individuals but not of celebrities, who seek to be known and recognised, or heads of government and State, who are identified with the country. For celebrities, it's the penalty of their fame. For political leaders, it's an inevitable consequence of their claim to represent the nation.

So back to my three questions. I'm afraid I don't have an answer to the first but Mr Modi's aversion to ties should be obvious. He prefers open neck shirts or even polo neck jumpers under his jacket. This is how he was often dressed in France and Germany. Indeed, there were occasions when every other man had a tie on—including the French Foreign Minister, who was accompanying him—whilst Mr Modi deliberately did not.

Now Mr Modi, the individual, has a right to dress as he wants. But do we have a right to expect something more from Mr Modi, the Prime Minister? To put it differently, it may be acceptable for an individual to be oddly or inappropriately attired but is it improper—even discourteous to his hosts—for the Indian Prime Minister to be wrongly dressed?

Before I come to the answer, two further facts need to be remembered. First, the occasions when Mr Modi was seen without a tie—at the Hanover Fair and the Airbus Factory in Toulouse—were public not private visits. They were part of his official itinerary. This means he was there not in his individual capacity but as Prime Minister of India.

Second, it's international convention and practice to dress formally on such occasions. All over the world that means a suit and tie. The Indian equivalent is our *bandhgala*. To defy that dress code suggests either ignorance of or indifference to a convention that is universally considered suitable. It could also imply a certain disdain for your hosts, who have meticulously observed the code.

Mr Modi's open neck shirts speak of a casualness and informality that is charming at a Sunday brunch or an afternoon stroll in the country but improper—even impolite—when flaunted by a Prime Minister for whom others have made elaborate arrangements, including the enforcement of strict protocol. This is why it's inappropriate.

And, finally, to my third question: Is this a suitable subject for public comment? Or am I wrong to criticise Mr Modi's choice of clothes and style? Frankly, that depends on what you expect of your Prime Minister and how important he is to the image of the country.

If the Prime Minister is the first representative of India then how he's dressed and what impact that makes affects the country. That's why even her opponents were proud of Indira Gandhi's sartorial style when she was abroad. It made us feel good.

On the other hand, if the Prime Minister doesn't matter then his sartorial idiosyncrasies are of no consequence. He can be as eccentric as he wants.

For me, however, Mr Modi matters a lot.

9

A Case of Two Donalds but One Quack!

Not so long ago the best known American called Donald was Walt Disney's lovable duck. Today there's also President Trump. I've been familiar with the comic book character since childhood. The other Donald is relatively new to me.

Let me, therefore, start with the original one. For those who don't know him he's a white duck with a prominent yellow beak. He usually wears a sailor's shirt and cap. Although he never wears trousers he always sports a bow tie. Along with his beloved Daisy Duck and three nephews, Huey, Dewey and Louie, he was a reassuring companion on hot summer afternoons in the 1960s and 1970s. We literally beat the heat together!

The Duck is some ten years older than the President but they were both born in June. I wonder if this is why they seem so similar?

Let me quote from Wikipedia's biography of Donald Duck. 'Donald is most famous for his semi-intelligible speech and his mischievous and temperamental personality...Donald's two dominant personality traits are his short temper and his positive outlook on life.' Would I be unfair if I said this could also be a description of Mr Trump?

Part of the Duck's charm is you're never quite sure what he's saying and often suspect he isn't either. As a portrait on BBC News states: 'The secret to his longevity lies in his distinctive—but unintelligible—command of language.' Most people would say that's equally true of the President. In Mr Trump's case, it's not uncommon to work out what he means despite how he has said it. In an interview earlier this month, the editors of *The Economist* were told 'we need reciprocality'. That's so much more impressive than mere reciprocity and certainly less likely to be forgotten.

In fact, the similarities run deeper. Wikipedia writes: 'The Duck gets a big kick out of imposing on other people or annoying them, but he immediately loses his temper when the tables are turned. In other words, he can dish it out but he can't take it.' Now, doesn't that remind you of the President?

But wait, there's more. 'Donald is also a bit of a show-off. He likes to brag, especially about how skilled he is at something...his love of bragging often leads him to overestimate his abilities, so that when he sets out to make good on his boasts, he gets in over his head, usually to hilarious effect.' Now, which Donald would you say best fits that description? I've quoted Wikipedia on the Duck but it could just as easily have been Washington commentary on the President.

Of course, both the Duck and the President are great achievers. The Duck has won an Oscar and played a major part in the war effort of the 1940s. Such is his fame, in Finland voters register a protest by marking the name Donald Duck. The President is, of course, a billionaire and, as Americans love to tell you, the most powerful man on earth.

Whenever they appear, both the Duck and the President dominate the situation but they're usually never alone. The Duck family includes Daisy, the three nephews and Uncle Scrooge McDuck. The President's entourage comprises Melania, Ivanka and Jared. He also has three sons but they're rarely seen.

Asked about his creation, Walt Disney once said: 'Like many large families we have a problem child. You're right, it's Donald Duck.' However, beyond Daisy there are no other female ducks in Donald's life. The President, as we know, is somewhat different. Not only is he a much married man but his affection for the female sex is legendary.

Of the Duck it's been said he's irascible when things don't go his way but he has a heart of gold and is devoted to his friends. Now, irascibility is not a quality unknown to the President and, at the moment, things certainly aren't going his way. But will we ever find out if he has a heart of gold or is devoted to his friends? Time could be running out.

Women In Power

1

The Iron Lady

I first met Margaret Thatcher in 1975. She was the upstart Leader of the Opposition, dismissed by Tory grandees as a mere Grantham grocer's daughter. Dressed in a bright canary yellow dress trimmed with a startling black band, she was hard to miss. Her voice was also rasping. The refined faux upper-class accent was still years away. Consequently, she caught one's attention but did not necessarily win your admiration.

Maggie Thatcher had come to the Cambridge Union as a special speaker. The University mood was dominated by the belief that James Callaghan's Liberal–Labour pact could deliver. The winter of discontent was three years ahead. At the time, the avuncular Prime Minister was both liked and trusted.

Impressions changed dramatically when Thatcher started to speak. There was something about her delivery that forced you to listen. There was a lot more to her content that made you sit up and think. But, above all, her passion and conviction stole the day. It was years before her economics won widespread support but the feeling she could make it to the top and even dominate British politics had already begun to rouse emotions both in favour and against.

At the time, I was a member of the Union's standing committee and got to meet Mrs Thatcher over coffee and sandwiches. Perhaps, I was overawed by her manner or lost in reverie but I recall her repeating a polite question I failed to answer. It was a casual inquiry about what I was studying and when I replied 'political philosophy', she harrumphed. 'Rather you than me,' she snorted. 'I prefer to get on with things!'

The next time we met, she was Prime Minister and had just won her third successive election. The coiffed hair, large pearl earrings and carefully, if artificially, modulated voice were firmly in place. She was, after all, at the crest of her political power. Thatcher's position was unchallenged.

I was part of a team from London Weekend Television at No 10 to record an interview. Afterwards, she invited us to stay for a beer and then, jug in hand, circulated around the room topping up glasses.

'Tell me, Prime Minister, when do you agree and when do you refuse to give an interview?' The question was asked by a young, redhead cockney spark. I'm not sure if he anticipated how it would stop her in her tracks but it caught the full focus of her undivided attention.

'That's a fascinating question,' she began. 'When I'm in trouble, when things are going wrong and people are questioning whether we've got the answers, I give all the interviews I can because I need to convince people that my government is in control and on target.'

'Oh,' replied the spark, assuming that was it and unaware there was more to come.

'Wait,' Mrs Thatcher continued, 'I'm not finished. When things are swimming along, when the government's policies are working and people are reassured, I shut up. Because, then, if I speak there's a good chance I'll put my foot in my mouth and create my own problems!'

That's one lesson our politicians could usefully learn. Stupidly, they do the opposite. But there are other lessons too like the case for conviction and courage, the determination to stay the course, how to popularise policies such as privatisation and her brilliant curbing of the unions by empowering courts to chase their funds.

I agree with David Cameron: Margaret Thatcher didn't just lead Britain, she saved the country.

2

Can Women Make their Own Luck?

Have you ever wondered why women in power can be so formidably impressive? Regardless of the correctness of their policies, they often display a steely determination, a cold, calculating, even ruthless belief in themselves. Faced with incredible odds, they can be almost frighteningly courageous. On such occasions, men might waiver or reconsider but not a woman.

Let me start with the example I know best. In 1986, when she was returning to Pakistan after years in exile, Benazir Bhutto knew it had to be with a bang. More importantly, she accepted that the impact had to be felt in the Punjab and not just her home state of Sindh. So, she chose to arrive in Lahore.

Sitting in first class, as the plane flew through the clouds, Benazir found her mind racing ahead to the reception awaiting her. It would be her moment of truth. In a mere matter of hours, she would either have a political career or it would be over before it had taken off.

The plane landed in a seemingly deserted airport. Benazir anxiously looked out but couldn't see the crowd of supporters she was hoping for. Silence and emptiness seemed to have shrouded the place. Was this the response she had evoked? Was this the end rather than the beginning?

At the bottom of the stairs were a few senior officials of the Pakistan People's Party. But that was it. No one else was present. The airport was empty. Her heart sank. '*Assalam Alaikum Bibi,*' her party's Punjab province president greeted her. He was smiling. So were the others. Their cheerfulness confused Benazir until they spoke.

There were lakhs of people waiting to welcome her but the authorities had not allowed them into the airport. They had sealed its precincts. Yet, just beyond, half of Lahore had turned up. Her return home was a triumph. She had defeated General Zia's efforts even though he was at the height of his power.

I witnessed the second example on television in 1980. Mrs Thatcher was Prime Minister of Britain. She was new and the Iron Lady image had not yet been born. At the time, she was under pressure to reverse her economic policies. With inflation soaring above 10 per cent and unemployment touching three million, even the pips had started to squeak.

It happened at her party conference in Brighton. Shortly after starting her speech, shouts demanding a U-turn interrupted her. Although such protests were not unusual, at the Tory Party conference, they were a sign her own party was against her.

But did Mrs Thatcher attempt to compromise? Or appease? Not for a second. As the shouting reached a crescendo, she interrupted her delivery, turned to face the protestors and delivered the most famous put-down in the twentieth century political history: 'You turn if you want to. The lady's not for turning.'

Today, this act defines Mrs Thatcher. It symbolises her determination, her defiance and her disregard of the odds.

The third example is one we've foolishly forgotten. It's from the 1970s when Janata party was in power and Indira Gandhi was isolated, unpopular and under pressure. A gruesome attack on Dalits in Belchi had horrified public opinion. With the country's ruling politicians too preoccupied with themselves to care, Indira Gandhi sensed her opportunity. She flew to Patna, motored into the countryside and then, because the monsoons had made the roads impassable, reached Belchi on elephant back. It was late at night and she shone a torch on her face so the villagers could recognise her.

The next morning, a stark black and white picture of Indira Gandhi entering Belchi, alone but undaunted, frail but fearless, her strong profile silhouetted against the black night, was on all the front pages. It signalled her return to politics. It also proved something more important. There was no one in Indian politics who could compete with her.

These are three women who had the courage to take their fate in their hands. They made their own luck and determined their future. Yet, the gamble each took could have easily gone wrong. If it had, two would have ended up as mere footnotes in history, whilst Indira Gandhi would never have overcome the shame of the Emergency.

The trick, I'm sure, is to know which opportunity to grab. The successful never get it wrong. The rest pick the wrong one and rarely get it right. But do women in power have a better strike rate than anyone else?

3

Sheila Dikshit

'Do you know the saddest outcome of the December 2013 elections?' In keeping with his question, Pertie looked rather glum whilst his voice lacked its usual booming stridency.

'Why don't you tell me,' I replied, wondering what he would say. Pertie's sudden interest in politics took me by surprise. Its continuation was perplexing. So I was curious to find out more.

'Sheila Dikshit! You only have to look around to see how much she changed Delhi. Whether it's the metro, buses or flyovers, the constant supply of power or just the cleaner air, the improved signages and refuse collection, today's Delhi is incomparably better than the city she inherited fifteen years ago. I would say Sheila was the best Chief Minister the capital has had and, probably, one of the best in the country.'

'So why did she lose?' I asked, 'In Madhya Pradesh and Chhattisgarh, the voters retained their chief ministers because they believed they had done a good job. Why did Delhi punish Sheila instead?'

Pertie's first response was a soft sceptical laugh. The sort that suggests I had missed an obvious point. When he spoke, his tone suggested he was speaking to a child.

'Sheila lost because of Dr Manmohan Singh's government. The anger that toppled her was not directed against her performance in Delhi.

It was seeking revenge for the corruption, policy paralysis and economic mishandling associated with the Central government. But Manmohan Singh, Sonia and Rahul Gandhi were not standing. Sheila was and she was felled in their place.'

'But that argument could apply to Ashok Gehlot as well?' I wasn't really picking a hole in Pertie's argument so much as questioning why he thought it only applied to Sheila Dikshit.

'In a general sense, yes,' he responded. 'But it applies much more specifically to Mrs Dikshit than anyone else. First, because she operated in close proximity to 7 Race Course Road and 10 Janpath. Gehlot didn't. And, second, because she's intimately identified with the Gandhi family. She, therefore, became a natural target for the anger directed at them.'

'So are you saying that Sheila Dikshit didn't deserve to lose?' That's clearly what Pertie's arguments appeared to add up to. It seemed his implied conclusion was that Delhi's voters had expended their wrath on the wrong politician.

'Let me put it like this,' Pertie began with a smile that suggested he had thought of a convincing reply. 'Suppose the Delhi elections had happened after the national elections and voters had already dispensed with Manmohan Singh and the Gandhis? Do you think they would have still bundled out Sheila or rewarded her with a fourth term to carry on the good work of the previous three?'

Pertie's counterfactual is certainly appealing even if not fully convincing. However, his underlying argument that Sheila Dikshit was defeated because Manmohan Singh and the Gandhis were not on offer, has the ring of truth. I've since discovered that several senior Congressmen, including a few top ministers, agree. Unlike Pertie, they don't have the independence—or is it the courage?—to say so publicly. But in confidential whispers they're speaking out loudly!

'We've lost a good woman,' Pertie concluded, the glum look back on his face. 'But that's democracy for you. The people's choice is not always the right one.'

I'm not sure how much consolation that will be for Mrs Dikshit. But I'm confident of one thing: History will be a lot kinder than this contemporary verdict.

4

Indira Gandhi

It was Indira Gandhi's ninety-seventh birth anniversary on 19 November 2014 and it brought to mind two questions: Was she a great Prime Minister or simply a long-serving one? And why is it that opinion polls repeatedly suggest she's considered the most successful?

Not being a historian I can't answer those questions with insight. Instead, let me present a few pertinent facts that could help you answer for yourself. But I warn you, it's not going to be easy.

Most people agree Indira Gandhi's high point was the Bangladesh crisis of 1970-71, which culminated in the surrender of East Pakistan and the creation of Bangladesh. Contemporary accounts suggest she had the wisdom to give Field Marshal Manekshaw the time the army needed to prepare as well as the skill to conduct a tireless campaign to win international support for India's stand. I doubt if many today would disagree.

Two questions remain: First, was she wrong to stop the war after the fall of East Pakistan? Many critics say she should have fought on in the west and finally sorted out Kashmir. I suspect if she had done so that would have invited international repercussions, including from our only supporter, the Soviet Union. It would not have been a risk worth taking.

The second concerns her handling of the Simla Summit where she trusted Bhutto's word only to be let down by him. No doubt it was an error of judgement but did she have an alternative? I think not.

If Bangladesh was her high point, the Emergency was her nadir. I don't believe Jayaprakash Narayan's call to the army and police to disobey illegal orders really threatened a serious law and order situation. Indira Gandhi was simply fighting for her personal political survival.

In her second spell in office, Indira Gandhi had to handle the Sikh unrest that culminated in Operation Blue Star. Was that the only course of action left to her or should she have attempted to force the militants out by cutting off access to power, water and food? It was a question raised at the time. The answer then was the same as the answer today; a prolonged siege could have created worse unrest in Punjab than a swift, even if failed, storming.

However, what's undeniable is Congress nurtured Bhindranwale as a tool to curb the Akalis and he turned into a Frankenstein's monster. The blame for that rests entirely with Indira Gandhi. She can't escape it.

Of her politics, you can say that her tight control of the Congress party decimated internal democracy and reduced India's oldest party to an appendage of the Gandhi family. More than Nehru, she started the tradition of dynasty. Thirty years after her death, Congress has to still struggle with both legacies.

Indira Gandhi's handling of the economy was perhaps one of her weakest points. She left behind the licence raj and a very tightly regulated economy. Successive governments, including Mr Modi's, are still trying to reduce the controls she thoughtlessly created.

Two facts, however, stand out above the contradictory impressions I may so far have created. First, the *goongi gudiya* of 1966 became the Empress of India in 1971, lost power in 1977 only to bounce back in 1980 and get assassinated in 1984. No other Prime Minister's career has had such dramatic highs and lows.

The second is that whilst she was superb at winning elections, she had little vision of what to do with the power she won.

Let me end by sticking my neck out. Hers was undoubtedly a horrible death but would Indira Gandhi have wanted to die of old age or illness? I suspect she would have preferred assassination to defeat or being forgotten in retirement.

5

Understanding Mamata

I've only met Mamata Banerjee once. It was fourteen years ago in 2001. However, that single experience could hold the key to understanding her wayward behaviour today.

Miss Banerjee agreed to give the BBC programme *HARDtalk India* an interview. It was fixed for 11.30 am on a mutually agreed date in August. It was reconfirmed repeatedly, including the night before. But these assurances proved to be illusory.

At the agreed time, the producer, Vishal Pant, reached Parliament to escort Miss Banerjee to our studio. She met him in the lobby and they walked out together. Then, just before they got to the waiting car, she said she needed to nip back inside and promised to return in a jiffy.

Vishal believed her and waited patiently. She never returned. For the first ten minutes, he thought someone must have detained her. For the next half hour, he thought something urgent had cropped up. But when a whole hour lapsed, he sensed she'd done a bunk.

So, Vishal went back into Parliament to look for the absconding Miss Banerjee. He found her surrounded by a group of Trinamool MPs. But when she saw him she refused to recognise him. It was as if she'd never seen him before.

Vishal feared he had a serious problem. Hoping that wasn't the case he decided to find out. He walked up to Miss Banerjee and touched her hand to attract her attention. He was anxious to get her to the studio as quickly as possible. After all, by that time she was nearly two hours late.

Miss Banerjee and the MPs surrounding her chose to misunderstand Vishal's gesture. They accused him of 'grabbing' her. They claimed he had 'misbehaved.' And, as he recalls the incident today, 'a minor scuffle' occurred. All because Miss Banerjee was determined to ditch the BBC without explanation, leave aside cause.

Despite his best efforts, Vishal failed to persuade Miss Banerjee to keep her word. She simply left the group and disappeared. This time she was gone for hours.

Thereafter, Vishal and our other colleagues launched a wild goose chase, following every lead, heeding every bit of advice, checking (repeatedly) every home or office she could have visited, but to no avail. They got no further sight of Miss Banerjee. Like the Scarlet Pimpernel, she seemed to have 'just left' each location where they thought they might find her.

The hunt continued for hours. Cars anxiously scoured Delhi. Worried phone calls were put through to every person who might know where she was. Alerts were mounted at her home in case she suddenly turned up. But Miss Banerjee had vanished into thin air.

Then, around ten at night, Dinesh Trivedi came to our rescue. A few weeks earlier he had persuaded Mamata Banerjee to accept. Now he felt a need to salvage the situation.

Dinesh asked Vishal to come to his flat in thirty minutes. An hour and a half later Vishal emerged with Miss Banerjee. The interview happened well after midnight.

It wasn't a great interview but the main thing is it happened. Miss Banerjee snarled and snapped. For a large part, she turned her head sideways, refusing to look me in the eye and giving the audience an angry profile to see. It was obvious she didn't care what anyone thought.

Now, tell me, do you recognise today's chief minister in this story? And do you think her mercurial behaviour is born of either insecurity or arrogance?

6

The Lady's Fingers

'Take a good look at her hands. She's bound to have long tapering fingers.'

This was how Ashraf bid me farewell. I was leaving to interview Condoleezza Rice. At the time (November 2001), she was Bush's National Security Adviser. Ashraf was the Pakistani high commissioner in Delhi. In the circumstances, it seemed a strange thing to say.

'What do you mean?' I asked. Ashraf can be elliptical but this was decidedly enigmatic. 'And how do you know what her fingers are like?'

Ashraf chuckled with glee. He was clearly enjoying himself. 'You obviously haven't done your homework or maybe, you know nothing about piano players!'

I have to admit he was half right. I wouldn't recognise a pianist even if one sat down beside me. But I still couldn't fathom his meaning. He was speaking in riddles.

'Condy is a professional pianist,' he eventually let on. 'Surely you knew that?'

I didn't. I had researched widely but this detail had eluded me. However, Ashraf, with his eye for the particular, had spotted it and was proudly flourishing his knowledge.

So when we met twenty-four hours later, my eyes focused on

Ms Rice's hands. They're delicate, even fragile-looking. Her nails, though unpolished, are perfectly manicured. And yes, her fingers are long and tapering. In fact, her hands are like the rest of her. You expect a virago of a woman but what you find is a gentle, soft-spoken, very feminine individual.

But thoughts of her piano-playing fingers were driven out of my mind by her combative and forceful responses to my questions. The lady, who a moment earlier seemed like a magnolia, had transformed into a warrior of steel. She continued to smile but her eyes were unrelenting.

It was two years later at a Washington Prayer Breakfast that I was again reminded of how central the piano is to Condy Rice. It was February 2003 and she was the guest speaker. Ashraf, by then the Pakistani Ambassador in America, was sitting beside me.

Describing herself as the daughter and granddaughter of ordained Presbyterian ministers, Ms Rice spoke of how in the 1980s she had drifted away from the church. 'Then something happened that I will always remember,' she said. What followed was an enchanting story.

'One Sunday morning I was approached at the supermarket by a man buying things for his church picnic. He asked me, "Do you play the piano by any chance?" I said, "Yes". And he said his congregation was looking for someone to play the piano at their church. It was a small African-American church in the centre of Palo Alto and I started playing there every Sunday. And I thought to myself, my goodness, God has a long reach—all the way to a Lucky's Supermarket in the spice section on a Sunday morning.'

The only problem was Condy was used to playing Brahms but at the church they expected gospel. Worse, the minister would start with a song of his choice and expect the musicians to pick up the tune. That, after all, is how Baptist churches conduct their service. But Condy was not used to this. So, how was she to follow the congregation? In desperation, she rang her mother for help. 'Honey, just play in C and they'll come back to you.' And they did! As Condy explained to the Prayer Breakfast, C is the foundational key in music and when people sing they always come back to it. Then she added, flashing the same smile I had first seen two years earlier and a wave of her famous hands, 'Perhaps God plays in C and that's why we always seem to find our way back to Him, sometimes in spite of ourselves.'

It was a touching but also a very humorous speech. There must have been over a thousand guests including President Bush and many members of his cabinet and they listened with rapt attention. You could have heard a pin drop except, of course, when loud raucous laughter replaced the silence.

As I heard her I realised there were two Condy Rices—the tough interviewee who refused to let me ruffle her feathers and the sensitive music-loving pianist who could soothe frayed nerves.

'Well,' I said, turning to Ashraf when the speech was done. 'What do you make of Condy Rice?'

'Better than Basmati!' came the quick reply. But I wasn't sure if it was a compliment or a joke. Ashraf's smile only added to the mystery.

The Price of Politics

We look upon politicians as scoundrels who have secured the best deal for themselves. Occasionally, however, that's not the case. There are some whose life is a story of tragedy. There are a few even, who have had to sacrifice the happiness of those they love most to serve the cause they cherish. This is the story of one such politician.

Over a decade ago, Aung San Suu Kyi left her husband and two young sons to fight for the political freedom of Burma (now Myanmar). Separated from their mother, Alexander and Kim suffered. Often, years would pass between visits to Rangoon to meet her. Understandably, emotional traumas followed.

Now more recently, Michael Aris, her husband, has developed cancer.[1] The Burmese generals won't grant him a visa to visit his wife. Instead, they want her to go to him. They believe they can thus force her to leave the country. She knows that if she does, they won't let her in again. So Michael, who has suffered a decade of loneliness, now must also bear his cancer without his wife's comforting presence.

Yet fifteen, thirteen, even twelve years ago, this was a happy contented family. I first met Suu when she was in Delhi as the Burmese ambassadress's daughter. At the time, she was my sisters' friend. I was too young to count.

---

[1] This article was published on 22 March 1999. Michael Aris passed away on 27 March 1999.

But I got to know her for myself when we met again at Oxford. She was married, a mother with a warm welcoming home. I was a graduate student and it turned out, a good babysitter.

'Michael and I want to go to the movies tonight,' Suu once telephoned to say. 'Will you babysit? I've cooked curry and rice and there's lots of chocolate cake. But watch out for Kim. His circumcision has turned septic.'

In between alternate helpings of curry and cake, I spent the evening cheering Kim whose unmentionables were in a hideous state. Poor boy. He howled and wailed and I could not even pick him up in case I made his condition worse.

In those days Suu laughed a lot. She was passionate, curious, full of energy, didactic, demanding and very, very correct. I once flippantly referred to the Chinese as chinks.

'Don't be silly!' she admonished. 'That's not even clever. It's just prejudiced.'

'All right, all right. Chinamen.'

'Chinese people,' she corrected me. 'It's time you realise what really lies behind colonial slang.'

Michael suffered when Suu, who had returned to Rangoon (now Yangon) to look after her sick mother, stayed on to lead the student movement. But he suffered in silence and he did so with enormous pride. 'You don't know how tough she is. House arrest simply doesn't bother her. I knew she was determined but her resolve is amazing.'

I suppose Michael had known or at least guessed that one day Burma would reclaim Suu. As Aung San's daughter, that was inevitable. But neither he nor the boys could have known it would feel like a return to the jungle—cut-off, beyond communication and contact, leaving just silence and darkness between you.

Yet, in the beginning there was idealism and hope. In the heady days before the 1990 elections, when Suu's National League for Democracy won three-fourth of the seats in Parliament, the deprivation, the separation, seemed bearable. A new Burma was being born and better days were definitely round the corner. It was during this period that I called her from London for an interview over the telephone for *The Times*.

'I knew you would find a way of getting through,' she laughed. 'Here I am under house arrest, no phones, no contact and you ring from London to do an interview. It better be a good one.'

Fortunately it was. Two years later when Michael published his book on Suu, the interview was included. It defines what she stands for, what the fight is all about. In it her voice is resonant, shining, clear. Dawn is just round the corner.

Sadly, it was not to be. In fact, many false dawns have come and gone and the Burmese long night has not ended. Instead, shadows have started to fall across the Aris family. Kim and Alexander have grown up but I daresay they have also grown away from their mother. It had to happen. Michael is ill, perhaps dying. And Suu is alone. No longer under arrest but by no means free.

When and if Burma returns to democracy, Suu will undoubtedly be at its helm. Her place in history is assured. Her contribution to it is beyond doubt. Michael, Kim and Alexander will always be proud of her. But how many will remember that to give Burma Aung San Suu Kyi, the boys had to lose their mother and Michael his wife?[2]

---

[2] This article was published on 22 March 1999. General elections were held in Myanmar on 8 November 2015 and Aung San Suu Kyi led her party National League for Democracy to an overwhelming win.

Wit On The Rocks

A Bit of This and That

The man beside me seemed to think he knew it all. We were together on the flight to Singapore when the airhostess asked him what he would like to drink.

'Scotch,' he replied and then added knowingly, 'Johnnie Walker.'

'Certainly Sir,' the airhostess smiled sweetly. 'Would Black Label do?'

It's considered one of the finest blended whiskies. It's also one of the more expensive. Most people would be delighted if it were offered.

'No, certainly not,' my neighbour shot back. He seemed strangely displeased. 'Red Label please.'

The airhostess could hardly disguise her surprise. I too was stunned. Red Label is a poor alternative.

'I'll see what I can do, Sir.'

Ten minutes later she returned looking flustered. There was no Red Label on-board. She apologised and again suggested Black Label or possibly, Chivas. She might even have offered Macallans. And, of course, there was a range of malts including most of the Glens. Lucky man, I thought.

'No,' my neighbour replied with firm finality, 'Red Label only.'

The airhostess disappeared into first class to see if there might be a bottle there. Meanwhile, my neighbour turned towards me and started to make conversation.

'I'm a comedian,' he began. 'I'm on my way to Los Angeles for a performance.'

'So was all that a joke?' I asked. Perhaps there was a punch line coming up. 'Or do you really prefer Red Label?'

'Those who know like Red Label,' he replied grandly. 'It's considered the best whisky in the world.'

And then, after a pause, he added, 'Black Label is only drunk in Third World countries. That's why they're offering it to us.'

He remained without a drink right through the flight.

***

I was in Singapore for the Asian Television Awards. This year one of the hosts was Cyrus Broacha. I can tell you that his humour had the audience in stitches. Afterwards, at the celebration party at Raffles, one of the guests could not stop talking about how funny Cyrus had been.

'I always knew that Indians are polite and gracious and your women very beautiful,' he started. 'But I had no idea you had such an amazing sense of humour.'

I smiled. But do we or is Cyrus a remarkable exception?

2

The Art of Being Witty

Have you ever thought about the uncanny connection between fame and wit? The famous or the notorious and often it's the same person, are frequently credited with a pleasing though perplexing sense of humour. Not of the 'ha-ha' variety but more literary. They turn their phrases with such cleverness that their aphorisms are remembered long after they are themselves forgotten. In fact, often it's what they've said that is the cause for their fame.

With the help of my late cousin Ranjit Sahgal and my colleague Amita Khurana, I have compiled a collection of witticisms that could be usefully purloined and passed on. I recommend them and if you use them, they're bound to impress.

The best often come from Winston Churchill. He had a style of saying things none of us can improve on. Consider this as a way of putting someone down: 'He has all the virtues I dislike and none of the vices I admire.' Or, better still: 'A modest little person with much to be modest about.'

Equally pithy and apposite was Oscar Wilde. Of an acquaintance he did not regard highly, he said: 'He has no enemies but is intensely disliked by his friends.' Of himself, he's alleged to have commented: 'Falling in love with oneself is the start of a lifelong romance.' Of those he disliked:

'Some cause happiness wherever they go; others, whenever they go.' By and large, its the British who have this wonderful knack for tongue-in-cheek humour.

It may surprise you to discover that Americans can be equally clever with their wit. Amongst the best is Mark Twain. Consider this: 'I didn't attend the funeral but I sent a nice letter saying I approved of it.' Or 'Why do you sit there looking like an envelope without an address on it?' But my favourite is this description of a friend by Forrest Tucker: 'He loves nature in spite of what it did to him'.

Now, here are a few you could bandy about at a party or cast in the direction of those you want to snub. Believe it or not, they were dreamt up by politicians. Talleyrand, Napoleon's foreign minister, once said of a woman: 'In order to avoid being called a flirt, she always yields easily.' Paul Keating, who was Prime Minister of Australia in the 1990s, said of an opponent: 'He is simply a shiver looking for a spine to run up.'

Occasionally, actors can drum up enough wit to say something memorable. Thus, Robert Redford: 'He has the attention span of a lightning bolt.' Or Mae West: 'Is that a gun in your pocket or are you just happy to see me?' And William Kerr, on a playwright who never cast him: 'He had delusions of adequacy.'

Even undergraduates can score points with their repartee. The Union Societies at Cambridge and Oxford are full of delightful examples. One of my favourites is this gentle dig which I recommend to our politicians. We would say of a particularly frivolous opponent: 'He is a very well-balanced man with a chip on both shoulders.' Or borrow from the good Reverend Spooner and call him 'a shining wit'!

Ultimately, of course, one has to return to Oscar Wilde. The sheer pithiness and incredible expanse of his wit is hard to beat. Just look at the sweep and twists of this random collection:

- There's only one thing in the world that is worse than being talked about, and that is not being talked about.
- I have nothing to declare except my genius.

- The only way to get rid of temptation is to yield to it.
- Work is the curse of the drinking classes.

Even incarcerated in Reading Jail, he said of his condition: 'If this is the way Queen Victoria treats her convicts, she doesn't deserve to have any.' And of a roué whose suspiciously deliberate indiscretions got on his nerves: 'I hope you have not been leading a double life—pretending to be wicked but being really good all the time. That would be hypocrisy.'

3

Wit and Whisky

Which is correct—whisky or whiskey? Actually, it depends upon what you're talking about. Whisky comes from Scotland. When it is made anywhere else, be it nearby Ireland or far away Japan, it is spelt whiskey. And as for the stuff they drink in America—bourbon or rye—that's very definitely whiskey.

However, Winston Churchill's delightful commentary on this product applies no matter how you spell it. My cousin Lakshman Menon has sent it to me. See if you admire it as much as I do.

> If you mean whisky, the devil's brew, the poison scourge, the bloody monster that defiles innocence, dethrones reason, destroys the home, creates misery and poverty, yes, literally takes the bread from the mouths of little children; if you mean that evil drink that topples men and women from the pinnacles of righteous and gracious living into the bottomless pit of degradation, shame, despair, helplessness and hopelessness, then, my friend, I am opposed to it with every fibre of my being.
>
> However, if by whisky you mean the oil of conversation, the philosophic wine, the elixir of life, the ale that is consumed when good fellows get together, that puts a song in their hearts and the warm glow of contentment in their eyes; if you mean good cheer, the stimulating sip that puts a little spring in the step of an elderly gentleman on a frosty morning; if you mean that drink that enables man to magnify his joy and to forget life's

> great tragedies and heartbreaks and sorrow; if you mean that drink the sale of which pours into our treasuries untold millions of dollars each year, that provides tender care for our little crippled children, our blind, our deaf, our dumb, our pitifully aged and infirm, to build the finest highways, hospitals, universities and community colleges in this nation, then my friend, I am absolutely, unequivocally in favour of it.
>
> This is my position and, as always, I refuse to compromise on matters of principle.

Now, I'm not sure how much of wit and wisdom is fuelled by whisky but after a drink or two, I would be prepared to wager a fair amount. Here's a collection of stinging quotations that enables you to be rude in style and carry the distinct odour of the Scottish tipple. Would you disagree?

- I've just learned about his illness. Let's hope it's nothing trivial.
  —Irvin S Cobb
- He has Van Gogh's ear for music.
  —Billy Wilder
- I have never killed a man but I have read many obituaries with great pleasure.
  —Clarence Darrow
- He uses statistics as a drunken man uses lamp posts for support rather than illumination.
  —Andrew Lang

And then there's this epitaph that could only have been crafted under the influence of whisky. But perhaps it is also a case of in vino veritas? 'Here lies my wife, here let her lie. Now she's at peace and so am I!'

Let me however, leave the last word to two comedians who know their whisky or whiskey. First, Ronnie Corbett, a Scot: 'It is true whisky improves with age. The older I get, the more I like it.' Next, WC Fields, an American: 'A woman drove me to drink and I didn't have the decency to thank her.'

4

Words, Words, Words

Who said Indians don't have a sense of wit? Trawl the net and you'll discover how inventive and clever we can be. But what has really surprised me is how good we are at devising puns and rhymes. In fact, our command of multiple languages and cultures makes the possibilities seemingly endless.

My cousin, Nalini, has sent me a collection of home-made aphorisms gleaned from the world of twitter. They were part of an infectious and exploding response to Swami Nityananda's expose in March 2010. There is a theme that runs through all of them; they poke fun at the twin lives of the Swami.

First, there are straight puns. As is conventional, these juggle around simple homonyms, i.e. two words that sound the same but have different meanings. However, in each case they're also placed in apparent opposition to each other.

The simple ones are: 'Missionary by day, missionary by night', 'Pray by day and prey by night' and 'Dear God by day, Thank God by night'. One step better are those that combine different cultures and languages to achieve the same effect. Here are a few: 'Ram by day, ram by night'; 'Bangalore by day, bang galore by night'; 'Holy by day, holi *hai* by night' and 'Swami by day, Show me by night'.

Next are the aphorisms that rely on a very apposite sense of rhyme. Once again, notice the cross-cultural and multilingual use of words:

- Sandalwood by day, Tiger Woods by night
- Monk by day, Old Monk by night
- Monk by day, bonk by night
- Renounce by day, pounce by night
- *Chamatkar* by day, *balatkar* by night
- Sri Sri by day, *Stri Stri* by night
- Shiva's disciple by day, Chivas disciple by night
- *Swahaa* by day, *Aaah aaaaaha* by night
- Moral by day, oral by night
- God-man by day, lay-man by night
- Discourse by day, intercourse by night
- Seer by day, leer by night

However, my favourites neither pun nor rhyme but rely on an inspired twist in the meaning. Some are astonishingly clever. Here are a few: 'Spiritual by day, spirited by night'; 'Saffron by day, blue by night'; 'Do-gooder by day, Good-doer by night'; 'Incense by day, incest by night'; 'Divine message by day, divine massage by night'.

But the winner falls into a category of its own. It relies on one of the world's favourite nursery rhymes but then pulls it apart only to put it together again in a completely different way with the meaning quite different to what our parents originally intended. Here it is: 'Baba by day, black sheep by night!'

Now if only Mani Shankar Aiyar had taken recourse to such wit, his description of Arun Jaitley could have met with ready smiles rather than protest. In response to being called a 'half-Maoist' by Jaitley, Aiyar referred to him in the Rajya Sabha as a 'full fascist' in May 2010. It's a tired and clichéd epithet and I can't see why the BJP is offended. It's certainly not Mani at his best.

Borrowing from the Cambridge Union, here are a few things Mani could have said: 'When it comes to Mr Jaitley's comments, it's a case of mind over matter. I don't mind and he doesn't matter!' Or, best of all: 'What can I say about Arun Jaitley? The poor chap's a sheep in lamb's clothing!'

5

Welcome King Freddy

26 March 2012: This morning I want to introduce an old and dear friend. We first met almost forty years ago. Then he was a tubby smiling school boy. Today he will be received as an honoured state guest and loyal friend of India. Senior ministers, the massed bands of the defence services and a twenty-one-gun-salute will welcome him.

Frederick Charles Uhuru Lullumbuwesi, named after the Kaiser and the Prince of Wales, is the Bagato of Burungundi and, as his seventeen titles proclaim, 'The Face of the Sun', 'The Lord of the Mountains', and 'The Chief with Fire in his Eyes'. His friends simply call him King Freddy!

The shorter name dates back to Stowe. When he arrived at the school he was accompanied by a retinue of Burungundian warriors with painted faces and ivory-handled fly whisks in their hands. 'Who are they?' he was asked by the incredulous third-formers. 'Don't worry about that lot,' he nonchalantly answered, waving the warriors away. 'They think I'm god!'

King Freddy used to be the most intelligent but also the laziest person I've met. He'd spend all day lounging on a rickety sofa in his study. But his essays were always alpha plus. Incidentally, his English was as flawless as the Queen's; his accent far better.

Alas, King Freddy's life has been less perfect. Whilst he was at Cambridge, his father, the then Bagato, was overthrown and savagely killed by the awful General Moses Ullumbawayo. For the next thirty years King Freddy languished in his Cadogan Gardens flat in London, occasionally dining at the Drones and frequently at The Wolseley, whilst the usurper ruled in Burungundi.

'He's done unspeakable things to the Palace,' King Freddy would lament. And indeed, Lullachi, the capital, once famous for its colonial villas with their manicured lawns and fancy topiary, was reduced to pot-holed roads and crumbling government buildings.

However, in 2003 everything changed. General Ullumbawayo died, suddenly and mysteriously. Perhaps it was an assassination or just an unexplained heart attack. As ambitious tribal leaders competed to succeed him, Burungundi succumbed to civil war. Lullachi was devastated although, miraculously, King Freddy's Palace of the Purple Flower survived intact. A ravaged and exhausted nation looked to its ancient but still-loved royal family for succour and King Freddy was asked to come home.

Next year King Freddy will mark his tenth anniversary on the Golden Bee Throne. Pictures of him sitting on it in a dark double-breasted suit adorn the capital's streets. In the last decade, Burungundi, a country locked within the borders of South Africa, has achieved one of the continent's highest growth rates, the lowest child mortality rate and an inexplicably huge consumption of pink champagne.

The restored Bagato has lived up to all the ancient Burungundian customs. He has six wives, although the only one accompanying him today is the one they call 'The Mother of the Eldest Son'. Little Georgie is, of course, following his father's footsteps at Stowe, where he's already captain of the rugger team and the school marathon record-holder.

When we meet this evening at the Rashtrapati Bhawan banquet it will be after a gap of fifteen years. But I can bet King Freddy will be wearing his trademark Saville Row doubled-breasted suit with a kerchief in his pocket. And when he rises to toast the President he'll grimace as he discovers it's only *nimboo pani*.

Welcome to Delhi, King Freddy – and happy April Fool's Day to the rest of you!

6

The Sting is in the Tail

Has it occurred to you that most of the wit you hear is borrowed from someone else? Few people are actually genuinely funny. They just purloin with great care, add a touch of their own and fail to give credit to the original speaker.

Now if you want to be witty, one of the cleverest ways is to use paraprosdokians. You won't find the word in the *Oxford English Dictionary* but it's in Wikipedia. It's a figure of speech in which the second half of a phrase is surprising or unexpected. The sting is in the tail!

I most enjoy paraprosdokians when they're used as a put down. PG Wodehouse's description of a fat woman is devastating: 'She looks as though she's been poured into her clothes and forgot to say "when".' So too Groucho Marx's parting comment to his hostess: 'I've had a perfectly wonderful evening, but this wasn't it.'

For debaters, paraprosdokians are a godsend. Here's one from the Cambridge Union which is a part of the conventional armoury used for tackling awkward opponents: 'Our differences are a case of mind over matter—I don't mind and he doesn't matter.'

Churchill was one of the few politicians who used paraprosdokians to great effect. Often, the United States was his target: 'You can always count on the Americans to do the right thing—after they've tried everything else.'

But even Clemenceau, though French, had a knack for it. And guess who his target was? 'America is the only country to have progressed from barbarism to decadence without experiencing the intervening stage of civilisation.'

There's a delightful but possibly apocryphal anecdote about George Bernard Shaw and Winston Churchill, which is entirely based on this delicious figure of speech. The playwright sent the politician two tickets to the first night of one of his new plays. 'For you and a friend, if you have one,' the accompanying note read. Not a bit put out, Churchill replied, 'I can't make the first night but I'll be there for the second, if there is one.'

If you like the risqué variety, here are two of them about men and women that might be a trifle sexist but are possibly true. First: 'Women will never be equal to men until they can walk down the street with a bald head and a beer gut and still think they're sexy.' Second: 'Behind every successful man is a woman; behind the fall of a successful man is usually another woman.'

Or if you're fed up of television, try this: 'The evening news is where they begin with "Good Evening" and then proceed to tell you why it isn't.'

Finally, my late cousin Ranjit Sahgal was a master of paraprosdokians. Here are some he used to great effect, often with me as his target:

- The last thing I want to do is hurt you, but it's still on my list.
- If I agreed with you, we'd both be wrong.
- A clear conscience is the sign of a fuzzy memory.
- Change is inevitable, except from a vending machine.
- I used to be indecisive. Now I'm not so sure.
- I didn't say it was your fault, I said I was blaming you.
- To steal ideas from one person is plagiarism. To steal from many is research.
- You're never too old to learn something stupid.

Happy New Year!

Sartorial Issues And The Barber Philosophers

Mr Sinkins' Buttons

It's the smile on his face that I always find welcoming. Unlike that of other salesmen, it seems genuine. Then, of course, there's his cheerful greeting. Finally, he's a repository of wisdom. In fact, I've never known him to be wrong. And that's what happened recently as well.

'Good heavens, Mr Thapar, how very good to see you!' Mr Sinkins was in the suit section of Gieves and Hawkes when he spotted me entering his side of the store. He seemed to be brushing non-existent specks of dust off the sleeves of a row of grey pinstripes. After years of knowing him, I can add that no one understands a suit better than he does.

'You're a bit early, aren't you?' he said, as he shook my hand. He had walked across the shop floor which meant our meeting took place near the casual jackets stand, adjacent to the tie section. 'You normally come around Christmas time, don't you?'

Sean Sinkins possibly knows me better than I know myself. We first met twenty years ago when I hesitantly walked into Gieves and Hawkes looking for a blazer. I had never shopped in London's Savile Row and was apprehensive. I wasn't sure if I was making a mistake. But taking my courage in my hands, I ventured in. Mr Sinkins was the salesman who attended to me and sensing I was a little ill at ease, was extremely attentive and full of excellent advice.

What impressed me was the way he talked me out of buying the blazer I had my eye on. 'It's not for me to say, Sir,' he began, before he ignored his own gentle disclaimer. 'But I don't think it's your size.'

He was right. It was both too long and tight. But only when Mr Sinkins pointed this out did I realise the fact. Till then to be honest, I was quite taken with the blazer. New clothes, particularly when you fancy them, can flatter to deceive.

On that occasion I bought nothing. But realising Mr Sinkins had saved me from throwing my money away, I returned frequently and never acquired anything without his approval. Over the years he helped me with suits, jumpers, rugby shirts and an assortment of jackets and ties.

This time, after we had exchanged pleasantries, Mr Sinkins seemed to disappear suddenly. It happened so fast I felt a bit disconcerted. I decided to look around the shop on my own but couldn't stop wondering where he had gone.

'Do you recognise this emblem, Sir?' Mr Sinkins was back and from the look on his face I could tell he had planned a surprise. As he spoke, he flourished a set of pewter buttons and each of them had the three-headed Ashoka lion.

'It's the symbol of the Indian state,' I replied, wondering why he thought I would fail this simple test.

'Not quite, Sir,' he responded, without a trace of triumph. 'Once upon a time this was the symbol of the Raj. If you look carefully, the bit of Sanskrit that your country has added at the bottom is missing.'

Mr Sinkins was right. This version of the lion-head symbol did not carry the *Satyamev Jayate* slogan. But that apart, it was uncannily similar. As soon as he saw it, Mr Sinkins knew I would want to have it.

'I found this set in our storeroom. We used to sell a lot of them, but no longer. I knew it would please you, so I put it aside.'

I bought the buttons at once. Now I need a smart new black *bandhgala* to wear them with. My old one will no longer do. It's too tight.

Oddly enough, Mr Sinkins seemed to have guessed that as well. As I finished my shopping and thanked him a second time for the buttons, he stepped forward looking as if he wanted to say something. I sensed he had advice for me.

'Might I suggest that the tunic you get made is classic in its fit, Sir,' he hesitantly said.

'Of course,' I replied. Although I knew better than to contradict Mr Sinkins, I couldn't resist asking why. So I did.

'Ah well,' and he smiled sheepishly. 'Since you ask, I should mention that after fifty, the best of us develop a paunch. You're about ready for one.'

I laughed but I knew he was right. Next time I visit London, I'm going to take a few old suits and ask him to let them out!

2

Oh, to be Bald!

I've always wanted to be bald. I know that sounds strange, but it's perfectly explicable. And no, I do not yearn to look like Yul Brynner or Telly Savalas. Nor do I wish to masquerade as the Dalai Lama. In my case, baldness is perhaps the only antidote to my crop of horrible hair. It's thick, rough and wiry. If left untended, it looks like a bush at India Gate. Most of the time it feels like steel wool. Even a hurricane cannot blow through it. Like concrete, it keeps its shape. And, unfortunately, it's about as attractive.

So, my dream is hair that blows in the breeze, thin, soft and straight. Hair that falls across my forehead which I would have to periodically sweep off my face. When I see others with hair that looks like that, I wonder why mine is so dreadfully different. Their lank strands fill me with envy. Like Dryden, I contemplate the rape of the lock.

But since this is not to be—and dreams cannot sustain for very long—my only realistic option is baldness. A smooth shining pate, perfectly round and beautifully shaped, without a single hair. Not black, not white, not of any colour. I've promised myself that one day I shall achieve this. Not at the hands of a barber but by God's good grace. And I wait patiently.

Meanwhile Pritam, the gentle and usually reassuring specialist—to call him a barber would deny recognition of his superlative talents—who has battled with my woollen growth for a quarter century, has come up with a unique explanation. He was cutting my hair—if that's the right verb—when he offered this gem of understanding about the profusion that adorns my skull.

'*Jahan tak mujhe in batoh ki samajh hei...*' he started ominously. Pritam is a philosopher at heart. He always sees the deeper issue that lies beneath each surface incident and illuminates it with the gravitas of a Sorbonne professor. '*...jo log ganje hote hein voh buddhimaan bhi hote hein. Aisa lagta hei ki unki akal itni tez hei ki baal bhi jhad jate hein!*'

As he spoke, he pushed his fingers through my hair. Clearly encountering stiff resistance, they got stuck almost as soon as they started. Even Dr Livingstone would have made better progress in the dense jungles of Africa. The conclusion was obvious and we both laughed.

I can't believe I'm the only person who hates his hair. As I look around, I can see hundreds whose crop is so unruly, or unseemly, or simply ugly that were they to see it, as others do, they too would yearn to be without. Perhaps they're more discreet, maybe even a trifle embarrassed. Or they probably don't know how to express their inner qualms. I—as you can see—put mine in print. But of one thing I feel sure; of people like me there must be more.

So why doesn't someone devise an elixir for instant baldness? A tonic that proudly proclaims: 'Use three drops daily and your hair will never dare to grow again.' Or what about this? 'Massage into your scalp and watch your locks fall away.' I'd buy bottles of the stuff. In fact, I'd keep it in storage in case it ever runs out.

It would only need Pritam's philosophical observations to guarantee that self-induced baldness becomes a rage. No one who hears him pontificate would dare to let his hair be seen. (Of course, women might be an exception but that's another story). And I feel sure Pritam would be willing to lend his services for advertising, for a fee of course but the cost would be minimal compared to the gains that could be made.

So do we have any takers? Will any of the movers and shakers, the captains of industry and the barons of enterprise, the geniuses who spot an opportunity and know how to turn it into a fast buck, put their money behind a guarantee of baldness? It's an opportunity to make your fortune and here I am offering it to you.

I appeal to L'Oréal, Grecian 2000, Godrej and Brahmi Amla hair oil, in fact, to be honest to all the companies who have invested time and effort to change the hair we have; now move on to how we can get rid of it. Forget your tired promises of everlasting growth, dismiss forever the lure of dyes and tints and banish the illusion of waves and false curls. Those are tricks that have outlasted their day. And, anyway, the market is saturated with them. The new game is to be the first to offer baldness.

And when you invent the secret, don't forget to let me know. Oh yes, and Pritam too.

3

Pritam, the Philosopher

'*Aap ko kya lagta hai, kya hamara moorkh to nahin banaya ja raha?*' Pritam's question took me by surprise. I've never doubted his wisdom but I did not expect him to be so clued up on the latest political developments. He asked his question as he started cutting my hair on the day the NDA government was carrying out a Cabinet reshuffle. At that point of time, none of us was certain what would happen. But Pritam, despite not knowing the finer details, had put his finger firmly on the nub of the issue.

'*Har che maheene sarkar ki shakal badal dete hein*,' he continued. He was wielding his scissors with deliberate concentration, a sign that he was also thinking carefully. It's a combination I've come to detect over the years. After all, I've known him for almost twenty and we meet at least once every month. '*Magar shakal ke ilava aur kuch nahin badalta. Kya public yeh dekh nahin sakti?*'

More than his content, it was the tone of Pritam's voice that made me sit up. His scepticism at once dispelled my journalistic interest in the revolving-door government. As he saw it, they were simply rearranging the furniture on the top deck but the ship itself continued to sail aimlessly. This, I presumed, was why in his eyes the redecoration did not really matter.

I put that to him. Surely, I asked, the type of people in government, their character and their reputation, are important? He smiled and, I daresay, indulgently. But he took his time to answer. I could sense he was chewing on his reply.

'*Samajhyega aap* heater *kharidna chahte hein. To kya aap khabsoorti ke bharose chunenge ya kamyaabi? Aur phir fayada kya hua agar dekhne layak ho lekin garmi na de. Aise* heater *ka kya matlab?*'

To be fair to Pritam, his dismissiveness was by no means restricted to the BJP or even the wider NDA. He tends to think the same of most, if not all, politicians. So whilst the rest of us are exercised by their image or their rhetoric, their behaviour or their alleged politeness, Pritam judges them rather differently. As far as he's concerned, it's their performance alone that counts. Will they do anything? And by his reckoning, most of them have not.

'*Agar hamare neta kuch badal sakte the, agar aisa sochte bhi, to kya mulk ki yeh haalat aaj hoti?*'

I struggled to think of an answer but quite frankly, I could not. So I stayed silent. The truth is that Pritam's attitude reveals how little the actual content of a government matters to those who are, and have good reason to be, disillusioned with it. What can one say to them?

The test—and it has to be the right one—is what has a government done. Has it delivered on its promises? Has it adapted the country to the changing world we live in? Has it identified solutions to our many problems and tried to implement them seriously and relentlessly? These may be obvious questions but the answer isn't always yes. That's been true of India for so long, most of us have forgotten the time when it wasn't. But Pritam broke my little reverie with a sharp comment about the present.

'*Jab inse tel ki* company *nahin bechi jaari to aap hi bataye konsa sona bech sakenge*?' This time I didn't even attempt to answer. Anyway, Pritam wasn't finished. He was only pausing for effect.

'Vajpayee sahab *kehte hein sarkar majboot hogi aur* Advani sahab *kehte hein ki* party *safal hogi. Magar kaise? Jab do-do* ministry *ek admi ko di jari hain to iska yeh hi matlab hei ki sahi aadmi ki kummi hei. Ya dusre nalayak hein. Aur jab che maheene ke andar* party *ke* secretary *badle ja rahe hein to kya pehli baar galti ki thi?*'

I smiled. How could I not have? But despite his wit, Pritam's point was simple. A government that changes itself so often is a government that doesn't know what it wants to be. And, anyway, it's not the appearance that counts but the performance. On that score he, at least, was not impressed.

Yet, Pritam's disillusionment went further although I was slow to realise that. There was also a message for the media. Maybe it was less clearly enunciated but it was equally sharp and telling. I squirmed when it began to dawn on me. Stop getting lost in the details and the speculation, he seemed to be saying. They are peripheral. What counts is what's actually achieved. But that is an area we journalists seem to be unable to properly focus upon. And when we do, we get sidetracked by personalities.

I walked out of Pritam's saloon shorn of more than just my hair.

4

What an *Aam Aadmi* Can Teach the Chief Minister if Mr Kejriwal is Willing to Learn?

Most people know Rajesh Kumar Singh as a young twenty-six-year-old barber at the Taj Mahal hotel in New Delhi. It's a job at which he's both efficient and courteous.

The real Rajesh, however, is a very different person. Born in Jamui in the bad lands of Bihar, his own poverty has propelled him to establish 'an NGO', as he calls it, to teach dance to children of similarly deprived backgrounds. Rajesh offers them a chance to nurture a talent and fulfil a dream. Dance gives them a glimmer of hope amidst the adversity and penury that is otherwise their life.

From his salary and without any support from another person, Rajesh contributes ₹30,000 a month to fully fund the dance school. It's now seven months old and has fourteen students. Half of them are regular and come every day. The others, when circumstances permit. But all of them you could say are children of a lesser God.

I recently learnt that Rajesh's school has achieved its first remarkable and heart-warming success. Sushil, a seventeen-year-old, has found a job as a dance instructor at a school in Ghitorni. To appreciate what that means, you need to know more about Sushil's background.

Rajesh first met Sushil at a public park. He was doing acrobatic stunts. But Sushil wasn't exercising. It was a desperate way to earn money. It was his last resort.

Sushil's father is a casual labourer who is often unemployed. The family depends on his mother who is an ironing lady. Sushil has two brothers. An elder one who is unable to find a job and a younger one, who should be at school but is not. The family can't afford it.

At Rajesh's school, Sushil's talent blossomed. His self-taught skill at acrobatics transformed into a talent for dance. As Rajesh explains, Sushil has a great sense of timing and a very flexible body. I guess he's probably a natural.

Now, a teacher himself, Sushil can help his mother feed and clothe the family. And yes, his younger brother can go to school. In fact, he's also going to start learning dance at Rajesh's 'NGO'.

In just seven months, Rajesh's school has transformed one young man's life. Undoubtedly, it will achieve many more successes in the months and years to come. This is why I am writing about it once again.

Arvind Kejriwal and his Aam Aadmi government can learn a valuable lesson from Rajesh's vision. They've promised to create 800,000 jobs. I hope they do but it won't be easy. Rajesh's 'NGO', however, offers a simple and more immediate way of taking poor children off the streets, teaching them a skill and giving their life meaning.

Dance may not conform with what politicians and economists call employment but if it comes more easily to the poor and unemployed, it could be the opening to the new life they've been searching for in vain. Whilst he strives to create the jobs he's promised, Arvind Kejriwal could usefully start with small but more direct ventures like Rajesh's school that offer an initial answer to a problem that otherwise may take years to solve.

Actually, it's even possible that sometimes the *aam aadmi* could have the best answers to his own problems. This might just be one such instance. Now, will the Aam Aadmi government listen and, more importantly, is it willing to learn?

5

When Your Problem Lies at the Bottom

'What's the most irritating thing that's ever happened to you?' The young lady asked. It was a casual question at a casual encounter but it brought back memories long forgotten. It's strange how an odd remark can set off a cascade of thoughts. Yet, that's precisely what happened.

What indeed, I asked myself. The problem is not just one of evaluation. It's also one of perception. Irritating is not annoying, it's certainly not infuriating but it's definitely more than just disliking. After all it's possible not to like but also not to care. Yet, you can't help but care about things that irritate you. So what exactly is irritating? I'd say it's being irksome. Something or someone that gets under your skin and will not stop 'irking' you until he, she or it goes away.

Amongst the most irritating things in the world are shop assistants who try to make you buy what you may not want or worse, may not even suit you. I realise that persuasiveness is part of their service but it has the effect of conning you into decisions that rationally you should avoid. I'm often taken in by their style and enthusiasm and end up with things I don't need, don't want and cannot use.

The young lady's question reminded me of an occasion when something similar happened although with a strange twist in the tale.

It occurred when I was in my early thirties. I'd received a surprise bonus and decided to blow it on a new suit. Feeling rather pleased with myself and eagerly anticipating the joy of buying something new and expensive, I walked into Burberry in The Haymarket. Sadly, this particular branch is no longer a retail outlet but in the mid-1980s it was. At the time it was also one of my favourite shops.

'What will be your pleasure, Sir?' said a needlessly unctuous shop assistant as I stepped in.

'I'm looking for a new suit or maybe a blazer and trousers,' I was spreading my bets because I wasn't sure what I would find.

'Ah,' said the man with an unnecessarily big smile, 'you certainly have the sort of figure that would look good in a suit.'

He meant to be pleasing but he wasn't. I know my good points and my bad ones as well and I certainly don't need them pointed out. So I ignored him and walked straight to the rack of suits at the back of the shop. I knew my way around Burberry well enough to do without his assistance.

After a bit I reached for a dark charcoal-grey pinstriped suit. It was double-breasted. I had always wanted one like that. Perhaps this was the time to buy it.

'Do you have this in size thirty-six?' I asked unable to find the right size myself.

The attendant busied himself checking through several suits before he returned. He had one that looked exactly right.

'Try this, Sir,' he said, 'not quite thirty-six but it's the next best thing.'

I was so happy to find what I wanted and so full of excitement and anticipation that I failed to realise the meaning of what the attendant had just said. As the finer details of his exposition escaped me, I eagerly dashed to the trial room to put on the suit he had recommended. It was the right material. It was the perfect cut. It was the desired colour and style. But, alas, it was the wrong size. It was thirty-eight and it hung on me. I walked out looking like a child in its grandfather's clothes.

'Not a bad fit, Sir,' said the attendant. 'A trifle long in the sleeve, a bit full in the chest and the seat could do with a little taking in. But in every other way it looks as if it's made for you.'

The mirror, however, suggested otherwise and though the attendant tried to persuade me to the contrary, I opted for something else.

This time my eye fell on a beige single-breasted gaberdine suit. As I took it off the rack I could visualise myself wearing it with a pale blue shirt and a bright yellow tie. That sort of contrast was all the rage in London in the mid-1980s.

This time the size was right. The problem was the colour. Indians, in case you haven't noticed, are themselves beige coloured. Consequently, a beige suit doesn't do very much for our appearance. It makes us look drab. Once again I walked out of the trial room feeling glum.

'If I may say, Sir?' said the attendant beaming from ear to ear. 'This is just the colour for you!'

'Is it?' I asked foolishly. I was stunned and did not know what else to say.

'Oh yes, Sir,' he continued. 'How shall I put it? It matches your skin.'

Once again the mirror took a different view and it wasn't long before I accepted that mirrors don't lie.

Finally, I opted for a grey herringbone sports jacket with rather fetching leather buttons and soft leather patches on the elbows. It was subdued but stylish and I fancied myself wearing it with a pair of twill trousers and a colourful silk tie or perhaps a cravat.

I quickly put it on. Since it was a jacket I did not have to visit the trial room. Once buttoned, I twirled in front of the mirror. It looked good. Very good. Until I got a glimpse of what it looked like from the back. The flap between the twin vents seemed to stick out.

'Oh dear,' I said, 'what's this?'

'What's what, Sir?'

'Why is the back flap protruding?'

'Beg pardon Sir,' said the attendant this time without his silly smile, 'it's not the flap.'

'Well then what is it?'

'It's your bottom Sir. It's a bit too big for the rest of you!'

I should have listened to him. I should have left the jacket behind and gone home. But I didn't. I was determined to buy something and even more determined to prove the shop attendant wrong. So I bought the jacket.

For the next nine years, it hung in my wardrobe. On occasion, I would take it out, put it on and like what I saw from the front. Then I would turn in front of the mirror and the protruding back flap would once again catch my attention.

Last year, I gave it to my nephew Vikram. He's my size in every way except his bottom doesn't stick out.

Portrait Of A Mother

1

Indrajit Gupta and Mummy

One of our failings is that we, Indians, judge a man by the sweetness of his tone. So, saccharine often deceives us. Conversely, a gruff voice and manner or eccentric behaviour makes us edgy. Many are the people who we have as a result misjudged. Indrajit Gupta, I suspect, was one of them.

I must have been eighteen when I first got to know him. Unaware of the fact that he was an old and close friend of my mother, I recoiled at the suggestion of a meeting.

'I've got Chingri coming to dinner,' Mummy suddenly announced one day.

'Who's he?' I said, and then trying to sound smart added, 'Or what's that?'

'That, young man,' she rebuked me, 'is Indrajit Gupta. I have known him since I was a teenager. He's also one of our better known MPs.'

Chingri, it turned out, was his nickname. In Bengali, it means little prawn. But, alas, at eighteen I was far too brash to appreciate such things. And since at the time he was only a member of parliament—his tenure as Home Minister lay decades ahead—I wasn't even curious.

Consequently, I wasn't pleasant company at dinner. I wasn't rude or surly, just uncommunicative. Eighteen-year-olds are so certain of their likes and dislikes that they can seemingly cut the rest of the world off. I did.

Yet, Mr Gupta—for that's what I always called him—did not seem to mind. Perhaps, he understood. I'm pretty sure he indulged me.

Years passed before our paths crossed again. Perhaps, I was careful to absent myself each time he came to dinner or maybe Mummy chose not to make a second spectacle of her silly son. In fact, I'm embarrassed to admit that I think the next time we met may well have been a few days after he became Home Minister. If there were meetings in between, I have no memory of them.

'Mummy,' I said, ringing from the office as soon as news of his appointment came through, 'is this Indrajit Gupta the same Chingri?'

'Yes,' she replied, 'and I suppose you now want to meet him!'

I certainly did. Suddenly Mr Gupta mattered. Of course I was by then forty and wiser but that can't disguise the callow self-centredness of my behaviour. It's possible that since then age has changed me but at the time I was unrepentant.

I rang his office in North Block. As Home Minister, officialdom would have thrown a protective blanket around him. Penetrating it was going to be difficult. A secretary took down my name and number and promised to pass it on to the Minister. I felt I had hit a brick wall. I did not expect my call to be returned.

An hour later, Mr Gupta rang. He dialled himself and gave his name simply as 'Indrajit Gupta'. I behaved like any other journalist. I congratulated him, told him his was the best appointment since Nehru became the Prime Minister and immediately asked for an interview. I wanted to get his first.

'Do I have the option of saying no?' he teased.

I wasn't sure what to say, so I said nothing.

'Bimla would never talk to me if I did that,' he laughed. 'When do you want to come over?'

Thereafter he gave me many interviews. The double we did the week the Deve Gowda government fell was electrifying. Sadly, its outcome annoyed him but the misunderstanding—for that is what it was—did not last. In the interview, Mr Gupta was candid to the point of being hurtful or so, at least, Mr Deve Gowda thought. But he spoke only the truth. Others hid it or denied it. He had the strength to face up to it, admit it and smile. That smile and his magical but mischievous eyes ensured that he never gave offence.

This January, whilst he was at the All India Institute of Medical Sciences, Mummy telephoned to find out how he was. Once again I was sceptical. I didn't think she would get through. Don't phone, I suggested, write a letter instead. Wisely she disregarded my advice.

'I'm going to come and see you, Chingri,' she said.

'That'll be a handful for the doctors,' he replied. 'Don't you think they have trouble enough with just me?'

He knew he was dying of cancer but that never affected his humour. To the end, he was irreverent and playful. The gruffness stayed too. But inside he was always soft and gentle.

'He used to do my maths homework,' Mummy suddenly said the day he died. She may have told me this earlier but I do not recall the story. Maybe I was still eighteen.

'I hated maths and he was damned good at it,' she said looking at his photograph on Star News with the years 1919-2001 written below it. 'I'd say, "Come on Chingri, I can't afford to fail again" and he would sit down at the dining table and take over. "But only this time, Bimla," he'd insist until, of course, the next time. The teachers at school could never understand why on some days my maths homework was so good. The rest of the time I was at the bottom of the class.'

2

The Army Way

I wonder if you realise how different things are in the army. Even though I'm a Rajasthan Rifles son, I often forget. And each time I acknowledge my mistake, I'm astounded by the contrast. We've grown so accustomed to the incompetence, grubbiness and ad hocism of Civvy Street that the efficiency, cleanliness and predictability of the army are hard to believe.

Last week my mother, an army widow, woke up feeling unwell. At eighty-seven that's not unusual except that Mummy is a tough old bird. Normally when she has a fever, her preferred cure is another cigarette and a long drive. She dashes off to the canteen to buy rations and of course, a few bottles of whisky! But on this occasion, she wanted to be taken to hospital. And that made everyone panic. If Mummy felt she needed a doctor, she must be serious.

The problem was that none of her children has maintained close contacts with the army. Mummy, of course, has but this time round she wasn't in a condition to help herself. So, as my sisters bundled her into the car and headed for the Army Research and Referral hospital (R&R), one of them rang Captain Sapru, the army chief's ADC, to tell him what had happened.

As I live separately I reached the hospital on my own, full of trepidation and mounting anxiety. I had never been to the R&R. I imagined it would resemble Ram Manohar Lohia hospital or at best, All India Institute of Medical Sciences. Actually, on a bad day, even Escorts and Apollo can be off-putting. They are often crowded and feel like railway stations!

I cannot tell you how wrong I was. The first remarkable difference is the atmosphere of quiet efficiency. At the R&R there are no crowds hanging around, no patients stranded in corridors waiting for attention. But there are a lot of doctors, silently, effectively and reassuringly going about their business. There was an orderly with a wheelchair waiting for Mummy and I can almost swear that as soon as she was placed in his hands, she started to perk up.

The doctors came promptly. They were knowledgeable yet considerate, thorough but also fast. Above all else, they kept smiling. And the hospital itself is clean, quiet and well-appointed. In fact, you feel better the second you arrive. To be honest, even though I was hale and hearty, I would have been happy to check in! Perhaps, it's a bit too tempting for hypochondriacs.

But it's the precision of army life that is most astounding. Nothing outside can equal it, not even that of the Prime Minister.

On the second day of Mummy's stay, the Army Chief came to visit. We knew he was coming but before he arrived, one of his ADCs telephoned to say he was on his way.

'The General will be there in seven minutes, Ma'am,' Captain Chauhan said. And he was. Precisely seven.

I was so astounded I kept staring at my watch in disbelief. I'm used to politicians who are late, even when they have no reason to be, and I had quite forgotten how punctual and punctilious the army is.

Later, I shared my thoughts with Mummy. I started by explaining how different the Army is to the civilian world I live in.

'You stupid boy!' she retorted. 'What on earth made you think otherwise?'

Since she was clearly feeling better, I argued back. She listened for a bit but then, assuming I was defending Civvy Street, cut me short. Her voice was steely.

'Stop it,' she said, 'you're arguing for the sake of it and you don't know what you're saying!'

It was at this point that a knock on the door announced the doctor. He came in smiling. I breathed a huge sigh of relief.

'And how are we this evening?' it was an innocent enquiry but the poor doc had no idea Mummy was all riled-up.

'Furious with this fool of a son,' she answered and then proceeded to tell him about our conversation in embarrassing detail. The doctor smiled knowingly.

'Anger,' he said sotto voce but looking straight at me, 'it's a sign of good health.'

For the next five minutes he proceeded to check Mummy. Her temper slowly subsided. Then, as he left, the doctor put his hand on my shoulder and added a word of advice: 'Don't overdo it. You might actually annoy her!'

3

Doctors with a Difference

'And how's the young lady this evening?'

It was Colonel Mukherjee. His cheerful greeting was aimed at Mummy as he entered the ICU at the Army's R&R hospital.

'Come off it,' she replied. But she wasn't being dismissive. She was pleased and bashful. Yet, a moment before, Mummy had seemed downcast. Twenty-four hours earlier, she had fractured her hip and the operation that followed had been tricky. At eighty-eight, general anaesthesia is not an easy option. Now, Colonel Mukherjee had made her smile.

'You're looking twenty years younger than this morning.' He reached out to hold her hand but before he could, she raised it to pat his cheek. Mummy adores flattery.

Watching from outside, I realised how lucky she was to be in the hands of such doctors. A patient-in-need cannot judge the quality of the diagnosis but the care and attention is easy to evaluate. Nothing is so reassuring as a doctor's manner. It's almost half the battle. The R&R has more doctors-who-care than any hospital I've been to. Like everywhere else, they're short-staffed and rushed off their feet, but they still make time to explain, understand and sympathise.

Mummy passed through the hands of many of them. First there was Brigadier BK Singh, the consultant orthopaedic surgeon. He had the daunting task of explaining to three anxious daughters and one overbearing son what the options were and the risks associated with them. Each of us had different, often contradictory questions but he patiently answered all of them and convinced us that his original suggestion was the right one. He even let us watch the operation on the television in his office. I found it macabre but mesmerising.

Colonel Moorthy, the anaesthetist, was less flamboyant but he has a way of signalling what he means with his eyes or his hands. Not once did he hide how risky Mummy's operation would be. Not just her age but her frailty and sixty years of smoking were part of the odds she faced. At times, his honesty might have felt disconcerting but it guaranteed trust in his judgement. Finally, when he wheeled her out of the operating theatre and into the ICU, he signalled with his left hand all was well. I knew he meant it.

Then there was the dogged persistence of Colonel Joshi, Mummy's surgeon. The day after the operation, he came to see her. Still in pain, she wasn't keen to cooperate. But Colonel Joshi knew exactly what to do.

'Lift your leg up, Mrs Thapar,' he said. Mummy ignored him. 'Let's see how you move your toes.' She didn't bother. 'Just once,' he pleaded. She remained implacable.

'All right,' Colonel Joshi responded, smiling as he spoke, 'then we'll have to do it twice tomorrow.'

Mummy immediately responded. 'Look,' she said, shaking all five toes in unison. 'Brilliant,' laughed the Colonel. 'But I'll still be back tomorrow!'

Whilst Mummy was in the ICU, I would visit late at night to check on her. I knew it was flagrant violation of the hospital's rules so on the first night I crept in ready to be repulsed and sent back. Sister Asha confronted me at the door. I froze.

'You're late,' she said. I was flummoxed. What on earth did she mean? 'Your mother had a feeling you would come and kept awake for you. Quickly see her so we can get her to sleep.'

I felt certain this had been said to reassure me and it gave me the excuse I needed to return each night.

At first it might seem odd that army doctors should be so sensitive and thoughtful. After all, those aren't qualities one associates with soldiers. But I soon discovered how wrong these perceptions are. The toughness of a soldier's exterior is not false or skin deep, yet, there's more to him than that. Soldiers are tough because they understand human weakness. It's an oxymoron that conveys the truth.

There's also a second explanation—the R&R is not a commercial hospital. It doesn't exist to make money. And whilst I know private hospitals do more than realise profits, the fact that profit comes into their calculations seems to affect the relationship with their patients. That simply isn't the case here. So, when an army doctor spends hours explaining little things or you accost him and take up his time, the one thing that never occurs to you is that you could end up paying for it. It makes all the difference.

4

When Jest is Best

You could say I've become an amateur expert on recovery! Having watched Mummy pull out of a coma and move slowly towards normality, I can tell you the surest sign of getting well is the return of wit and humour. When a patient starts cracking jokes, he or she is on the mend.

'Morning Mummy,' I said the other day as I walked into her room in the Army R&R Hospital. 'How are you feeling today?'

She stared back with a querulous look on her face as if I'd asked a stupid question. 'I've got a tube up my nose and my hands are tied to the bed. That apart, I'm on top of the world!'

I wonder if she realised how happy her children were to hear her satirical response. We assumed it was a sign she was returning to her old self. However, later that day, when perhaps sleep made her dopey, I panicked in case she was relapsing. So, I unleashed a fusillade of questions to test her alertness.

'How many fingers?' I asked, waving my right hand. Mummy kept silent. 'What's your name?' I said, attempting a different tactic. Still no response. 'Who am I?' I continued, a little desperate. This time she slowly opened her eyes and shot back: 'If you don't know at your age, you've got a problem Sunny Jim!'

After Mummy had established a reasonable foothold in the world of consciousness, the next test was eating. The doctors were keen to remove the Ryle's tube but wanted to see a capacity to eat on her own before they took this step.

'I hope you're going to eat properly?' I asked, unaware of the ambiguity of my question.

'What do you mean?' she replied, almost offended. 'I always eat properly.'

'No, I meant I hope you'll eat with your mouth.' But my clarification only made matters worse. 'Are you suggesting I've been eating with my feet?' We dissolved into laughter but Mummy wasn't finished. Five minutes later, she reached for my hand and petting it to take the edge off her comment, said: 'You ask the most foolish questions. It's not right at your age.' I'm not sure if that wasn't a put-down.

'She's cracking jokes all the time,' I said to Colonel Bhattacharya, Mummy's doctor. I was looking for confirmation this was a positive development. His answer explained what I had intuitively sensed.

'It's a sign of many things. First, of mental alertness. Second, of wanting to participate. And third, of feeling happy.'

But I think I'm in a position to add a small footnote to the chapter on patient behaviour during recovery. The stage after wit and humour is what I call refusal to perform. It's another, perhaps stronger, sign of self-assertion.

In Mummy's case, it occurred when we were playing a little game. I would voice the first line of a nursery rhyme and she would say the rest. After Baba Black Sheep, Hickory Dickory Dock and Little Miss Muffet, I tried The Grand Old Duke of York. That's when it happened.

'I'm not a performing monkey, you know,' and with that she sealed her lips and shut up. No matter what I said, she wouldn't speak. At least not until I started a more adult line of conversation.

Now, as Mummy gets better, I have to watch what I say.

5

Never Say Die

I know this sounds strange but there's a lot you can learn sitting by the bedside of the seriously ill. Both Mummy and my brother-in-law, Irwin, are in hospital. Mummy is at the Army R&R Hospital, Irwin at the Max in Saket. The rest of the family and I seem to be in both!

First, I did not realise how brave the ill can be. Nor would I have imagined that *they* would make an effort to put *you* at ease when you meet them. Yet, that's what happened after Irwin was told he has a fast-growing liver cancer. I met him with trepidation. I wasn't sure what to say and frankly, I was dreading it.

'Hi, Irwin,' I said, projecting a false cheerfulness. 'How are you feeling?' No sooner had I spoken than I realised that was a stupid thing to say. But Irwin burst into a big smile and his eyes twinkled with wickedness.

'Both the cancer and I are doing very well.' And then he added with quiet determination: 'I'm okay. Don't worry. You've got me to contend with for quite a while!' That was eight weeks ago. Although he's steadily got weaker and visibly less well, Irwin's humour has not disappeared. When the hospital put a tube in his stomach because he wasn't eating, he commented: 'From a loud mouth to a man with two mouths. That's progress!' When he couldn't shave himself and needed help, he said he kept a beady eye on the attendant: 'If his hand slips, it's my wretched throat that could get slit!'

Alongside bravery, there is their indomitable will to live. Last week, as I watched over Mummy initially lying helplessly in what her doctors called a precoma, I feared we were losing her. At ninety-two, age is against her. So too her obvious frailty. But Mummy is determined not to give up. She kept struggling back to alertness. And each time she did, my three sisters and I tried to stimulate her with conversation.

'Who am I?' I asked on one such occasion. 'My son,' she mumbled. 'What's my name?' I continued. 'Karan,' she muttered. 'What's your name?' I added. 'Bimla' But she was growing weary. 'How many sisters do I have?' This time I had pushed my luck too far. 'Oh shut up!' she said, fed up of my silly questions and went back to sleep.

There were times when Mummy was a frightening sight to behold. After exhausting all the veins on her hands and feet, the intravenous drip finally found a home in her jugular vein. Inches away, a Ryle's tube shared her nostrils. To prevent her yanking them out, the R&R Hospital sisters tied her hands to the sides of the bed. Yet, even from this restricted position, when asked by the doctors how she felt, she once promptly replied: '*Chalti ka naam gaadi*'. And then, in case Brigadier Nair and Colonel Bhattacharya do not follow Hindi, translated: 'Getting along nicely, thank you!'

Who would think that visiting Mummy and Irwin can at times prove uplifting rather than depressing? Whatever the situation, their spirit remains defiant. Of course, they have bad days and then your own spirits sink. But if you learn to see the fight they're waging, you can also feel the clouds lift, even if temporarily. At times it's sheer will that keeps them going.

It makes me wonder why we, who are well, so often give up.

6

Mother Knows Best

She was staring intently at the television when I walked in. The look on Mummy's face suggested bewilderment. I could tell she was displeased with something she'd heard.

'What's grabbed your attention?' I said, trying to snap her concentration with a little deliberate levity.

'It's the judges,' she replied gravely. 'They seem to think they know how to run the army better than the Army Chief! They want to force him to take in women officers. On the other hand, he's reluctant to do so. Surely this is something the man should be allowed to decide for himself?'

Even at ninety-three, the issue had riled Mummy. First as a wife and then as a widow, she's spent over seven decades connected with the army and firmly believes she understands it better than most. Judges, who have no martial tradition to boast of and little understanding of the services, are unlikely to change her mind. And Mummy can be pretty obstinate.

'Don't you think women have a right to join the army if they want to?' It wasn't so much a serious question as an attempt to engage her in conversation. But Mummy saw it as an opportunity to teach me a thing or two.

'Don't be silly,' she shot back. 'No one has a right to join the army. It's not a birthright conferred on you. Not unless you qualify and you are accepted. In this case, the army is the best judge of what they want and who meets their standards or requirement.'

'Oh come, Mummy,' I responded, still trying to be jocular despite her heavily crossed eyebrows and the visible irritation on her face. 'Don't you think women in uniform parading down Rajpath would make a fetching sight?'

I think she snorted. At least it sounded like that. At any rate, her contempt for my comment was difficult to miss.

'But the judges aren't only talking of decorative roles. Would you feel safe if the defence of India was left in the care of women fighting in hand-to-hand combat with strapping lads from China and Pakistan?' Mummy waited for the import of her question to sink in. When she thought it had, she delivered her coup de grâce. 'When you're faced with the prospect of ending up as chop suey or burra kebab, I think you'll be very grateful for a tough male soldier ready to sacrifice his life for you!'

The force of that rejoinder took me aback. I had no idea Mummy had such strong and passionate views. But now that I had made this discovery, I was keen to find out more.

'But there are non-combat roles women can perform. What's wrong with that?'

'If only you'd use your head you'd realise non-combat roles are meant for the second rank. Do you want women to be in a position where they are permanently inferior?' This time Mummy positively spat out her words. So I decided to change track.

'And do you agree with the argument that soldiers don't like taking orders from women? The army says it goes against their cultural grain.'

'It depends upon which women you mean. They may not like being commanded by one but they'll bloody well do as they're told when spoken to by a senior officer's wife!' Clearly that must have brought back happy memories because Mummy started smiling.

'Now enough of this nonsense or I'll think you're as daft as those silly judges.'

7

Mummy @ 94!

I hope you'll forgive a little self-indulgence but Mummy celebrated her ninety-fourth birthday yesterday and it's not every day that the Mater reaches such a venerable age. What makes this landmark even more special is that last week she was in hospital for a surgical procedure under anesthesia. As they wheeled her into the operating theatre, Mummy turned to my sisters and me and said, 'I hope the doctor knows it's my birthday next week!'

Mummy's always been a fighter with a sharp turn of phrase and a keen sense of repartee. 'How are you feeling?' I said, once the operation was over. 'As well as can be expected,' she slurred. 'And what does that mean?' I further questioned. 'Don't be stupid,' she shot back and ended the conversation with a distinct harrumph.

At her age, recovery is not a simple and straightforward process. On good days, she would sit propped up against the pillows, the centre of all attention. But if the conversation drifted to subjects that did not interest her, she would use unique ploys to steer it towards areas she prefers. A favourite was what I call the dancer's trick. Suddenly Mummy would start moving her head and eyebrows in an almost perfect Bharatanatyam *attami* with *bhruchalan*. It was a showstopper.

'You aren't cocking your right eyebrow as clearly as the left,' one of my sisters pointed out. 'I know,' Mummy said, 'I must work on it. I'm a bit out of practice!'

The other attention-grabbing trick was to say something that would freeze all conversation. Suddenly, she would raise her coffee or soup cup and say cheers. She would then take our enthusiastic response as a cue for one of her favourite toasts: 'Here's to you and Blighty, me in my pyjamas and you in your nightie!'

'Where did you learn that?' I asked.

'From your father. He taught it to me just after we got married. I was twenty-one at the time.'

On her bad days, my attempts to stimulate her and kick-start a conversation often got on her nerves. On one occasion, when I was playing the fool in the hope that might strike a chord, she turned towards me and sternly admonished: 'You know at your age, it isn't very clever to say such stupid things!'

However, whenever the doctors and nurses walked in, Mummy would perk up. She'd hold on to Major General Varma's hand and refuse to let go. Even in her nineties, Mummy hasn't forgotten how to flirt! Or she'd tease Brigadier DV Singh and insist he sing for her. The pun on his surname was delivered with a glint in her eye. 'Do come again,' she'd say when, finally, they were allowed to leave. 'And next time bring me some cigarettes!'

The night-duty sisters were Mummy's postprandial companions. By then the family would have gone home and she'd spend hours gossiping with them. She'd listen intently as they spoke about their careers and children. In turn, she'd spin stories about her childhood and, of course, her 'darling son'.

When it was time to leave the R&R Hospital, Mummy, as usual, was hesitant to go home. 'I quite like it here. They're very good to me.'

As the car entered the gate and progressed up the drive, Mummy stared at the house. 'This looks very familiar. Where've you brought me?'

'Home, Mummy,' my sister Premila trilled.

'I thought as much. The damn thing never changes!'

8

Remembering Mummy

Mummy's was a long, eventful and fulfilling life and she loved every moment of it. For her the cup was far more than half full. It was usually brimming, except if it was a cup of wine she would make sure she drained it to the dregs. No doubt her life had its share of ups and downs but she was an optimist who never looked back. I don't think she was ever depressed.

Twenty-five years ago, when she was in her seventies, she said to her grandchildren: 'I've hidden a couple of bottles of champagne and no doubt you'll find them when I'm gone. But I don't want you to just drink them. You have to toast me as well.' But then she got fed up and finished the champagne herself!

Mummy was born into a very different world to the one she departed on Good Friday. In 1917, there was a Tsar in Russia, a Kaiser in Germany and a King Emperor ruling India. Jallianwala Bagh was two years away and Mohandas Karamchand Gandhi was only a lawyer recently arrived from South Africa. Ninety-eight years later, America has a black President, we're proud to have a *chaiwallah* as our Prime Minister and though Britain still has a Queen, so do a lot of other countries but most of them were born boys.

Of her many qualities, there are three that capture Mummy's spirit and style. Hers was a warm and outgoing personality that knew how to break the ice. General Malik, our former Army Chief, tells me that on an occasion when he welcomed her by shaking her hand, she promptly responded: 'Ved you've known me long enough to kiss me on the cheek! And don't worry I don't use nasty cosmetics!'

The second quality that defined Mummy was her determination. She was a fighter and usually got what she wanted. A few years ago, after she had broken both her hips and was wheelchair-bound, my sister Premila was roused at two in the morning by the sound of feet shuffling in the dark. 'Christ,' she thought, 'we've got intruders.' But when she switched the bedside lamp on, she discovered Mummy leaning against the wall. 'Baby,' Mummy said, 'do you by any chance have a fag?'

The third quality was her style. It was entirely unconventional. She did exactly what she wanted and didn't care what others thought. In her seventies, she would drive a blue ambassador, which she called her blue bird, with an old cotton jacket over her right arm because she hated the sun, tattered gloves because she didn't trust the steering wheel and a cigarette between her lips.

Premila remembers an occasion when Mummy was driving down the Chattarpur road and the police tried to stop her. The closer the police came the faster Mummy drove until a red light forced her to stop. This gave the policeman the opportunity to approach her. 'Madam,' he said, '*mein apko batana chahata hoon ke aap ka darwaza khula hein aur aap mujhse race laga rahi hein*!'

Years later, when her memory was no longer reliable, Mummy showed great style covering up. One afternoon, when I dropped in to see her, my excuse for leaving was I had to get back to work. 'What work do you do darling?' 'Oh dear,' I thought, 'she doesn't remember!' 'I make TV programmes,' I said. 'Ah,' she replied recovering her wits in a flash, 'does anyone watch them?'

Mummy was also the most understanding and liberal person I knew. In 1992, when my nephew Siddo decided to tell the family he was homosexual, Mummy was the first person he spoke to. 'Nani,' he said,

'I'm gay.' 'So am I darling,' she replied unaware of what he meant. 'Nani, I mean I'm homosexual.' 'Well, so what?' she replied. 'You're still my grandson and that's what counts.'

Once, when I was a child and she was unwell, I said I would lock her in the bathroom and nothing would happen to her. Last week, I discovered the bathroom door was not as impregnable as I thought and God's reach was stronger than my protection.

Appendix

Can You Trust a Newspaper?

'Just because it's in a newspaper doesn't mean it's true,' my friend Aftab Jafferjee has always maintained. He first pronounced his verdict in 1982. At the time he was a young but upcoming lawyer. I was a rookie reporter on *The Times*.

'Quite frankly,' Aftab continued, 'journalists often make it up and they have no qualms about doing so.'

'Nonsense,' I answered bristling with self-righteous indignation. Fresh recruits can defend their new profession with a passion which in later years often seems misplaced.

'I'm sorry KT,' he replied, 'but I don't care what you say. I'll never believe everything I read in a newspaper. After all, I know how you can add *mirch-masala* to make a better story!'

Last week I realised how right Aftab was. It was a defining moment of truth. But what made it particularly shocking was that it happened when I read something published in a paper I hold in high esteem and regularly write for. It happened, unfortunately, on the pages of the paper you hold in your hands this Sunday morning. And if it could happen to me—when I know the proprietor, the editor and several of the journalists—it could quite easily happen to anyone of you.

The incident is connected to the interview I recently did with Kapil

Dev for the BBC and specifically to the fact that details of the interview and pictures of Kapil in tears were published in several papers including the *HT*'s front page on Sunday the 7th.

In a nasty piece in the *HT Diary* on the 11th, which was conveniently published without a byline, the paper asks, 'Why were photographers invited to the shoot and not stopped from clicking when the shoot was on? If you go by the book no photograph can be taken when a programme is being recorded.' The paper suggests—albeit in different language—that this was irregular and improper. It then asks, 'So who invited the press and arranged the publicity blitz?' The answer the paper offers is: 'Apparently, it was Thapar himself.' Finally, but with its tongue firmly embedded in its cheek, it concludes that 'there's no better master of self-promotion in the business.'

Not a word of this is true. Worse, the paper knows that to be the case and its own correspondent and photographer are proof that I'm right and the paper totally and completely wrong.

Let me explain. The *Hindustan Times* photographer was at the shoot but he was invited by Genesis, the BBC's public relations agency, and not by me. I was not aware of his presence until the interview was over and then only because he introduced himself. He did so because he wished to tell me that he would ensure a huge spread the next day and by giving advance notice of this he was also, I presume, claiming advance credit. Secondly, the photographer, HC Tiwari, was in the production room one floor above the studio right through the entire recording. He was not present on the studio floor and far less was he taking photographs as the interview was happening. Thirdly, the photographs Mr Tiwari took and which the *HT* published on Sunday the 7th were taken off the television screen after the interview was over. You only have to look at them to realise how obvious this is.

(Incidentally, this is also true of the pictures released by PTI and which were used by many other papers in the country. A VHS of the interview was given to PTI by Sunil Kalra of Genesis and, once again, PTI took their pictures off the screen. Again I had nothing to do with it.)

Now to turn to the actual report of the interview carried by The *Hindustan Times*. Once again the truth is quite different to what the *HT Diary* claims. The paper's correspondent, a certain Siddhartha Saxena, who wrote about the interview on the front page on Sunday the 7th, was given a VHS several hours after the interview was over. Again, the tape was given by Sunil Kalra of Genesis and I was neither consulted nor informed. In fact, the irony is that I quarrelled with Sunil because I thought the *HT* should not have been given a tape. But that's another matter.

Actually, to give Mr Saxena his due, he makes this clear in his article when he writes of 'an exclusive viewing of the interview made available to this correspondent'. Quite clearly, he wasn't present at the recording and it had to be 'made available' to him. If only the *HT*'s diarist had asked him!

(Once again much the same is true of the report of the interview put out by PTI and carried by all the other papers. Sunil Kalra delivered a VHS to Mr Jagannath Rao, their Sports Editor. The authorisation to do so was communicated to him directly by the BBC. I may have been an interested party but I was not involved nor do I have the right to instruct Sunil in this matter.)

So, what does all of this mean? Firstly, that the *HT Diary* is completely wrong. Secondly, that it is written with obvious and intended malice. Thirdly—and most sadly—if the *HT* diarist had wanted, he or she could have verified the facts by simply speaking with the paper's photographer and/or correspondent. By not doing so—which I presume is what happened—he or she has shown his or her cavalier attitude to the truth as well as his or her blatant intention to twist and distort it.

Of course the *HT* is not alone in behaving like this. Most papers—if not all—make similar mistakes. In fact to call them a mistake is a misnomer. Mistakes are usually accidental and what we are talking about are irresponsible if not actually intended errors. The only difference is that some papers commit these lapses more often than others.

So, Aftab, eighteen years later I must admit you're right and I was wrong. I can see you smiling with obvious satisfaction. In fact, even if you're gloating, you have every right to.

Yet, if this article is published exactly as I have submitted it, then I'll add one further thought—that would be an example of both a newspaper and of journalists making amends. And what might that be the result of you may ask? Guilt, contrition or clever public relations? My answer is simple although yours may be different. If this piece is published without alteration I will consider all wrongs to have been rectified or, at least, forgiven. And there the matter will end.

Now, wouldn't that be a small point in favour of newspapers? Be honest, Aftab.

This is an unpublished article written for 14 May 2000.